zero
waste
fashion
design

Bloomsbury Visual Arts
An imprint of Bloomsbury Publishing Plc

50 Bedford Square   1385 Broadway
London   New York
WC1B 3DP   NY 10018
UK   USA

www.bloomsbury.com

BLOOMSBURY and the Diana logo are trademarks
of Bloomsbury Publishing Plc

First published 2016
Reprinted 2017

British Library Cataloguing-in-Publication Data
A catalogue record for this book is available from the British Library.

ISBN:
PB: 978-1-4725-8198-3
ePDF: 978-1-4725-8199-0

Library of Congress Cataloging-in-Publication Data
Rissanen, Timo.
Zero waste fashion design / Timo Rissanen and Holly McQuillan.
pages cm
ISBN 978-1-4725-8198-3 (pbk.) -- ISBN 978-1-4725-8199-0 (epdf)
1. Fashion design. 2. Clothing trade--Waste minimization. I. McQuillan,
Holly. II. Title.
TT507.R57 2015
746.9'2--dc23
2015007422

Designed by Evelin Kasikov
Printed and bound in India

zero waste fashion design

timo
rissanen

holly
mcquillan

Bloomsbury Visual Arts
An imprint of Bloomsbury Publishing Plc

BLOOMSBURY
LONDON · OXFORD · NEW YORK · NEW DELHI · SYDNEY

TABLE OF CONTENTS

PREFACE

Ten years ago when we first started working on these ideas, we were working in isolation. We didn't know each other or know there was a name for what we were doing, and as a result we spent a long time struggling to both articulate our intentions and motivations, while attempting to visualize them through clothing. The successful future of fashion requires the building of community and sharing. So over the course of ten years that is what has begun to happen.

We hope that in writing this book you will be provided with an insight into this community, to ease what was for us a long and at times challenging process. That process was part excavation of history, part contemporary reimagining, and part call to arms for the future of fashion. This book explores zero waste fashion from all these perspectives, tracing the origins of respect for materials, outlining the case for a contemporary love of cloth and all those involved in fashion's physical and cultural production, all while demanding change.

There is no one way of doing zero waste fashion design. Although we are writing this book as a singular voice, our working methods are often very different. Our aim is to embrace this diversity of practice throughout the book.

For downloadable patterns from the book please go to www.bloomsbury.com/rissanen-mcquillan-zero-waste and follow the link to the online resources.

Facing page: Long Coat and Wrap Skirt from Holly McQuillan's Make/Use V2 project (2015). Photography by Bonny Stewart-MacDonald.

zero waste fashion design from history to now

Fashion is seductive, glamorous, even magical. Yet the industry and the garments it produces are full of inefficiencies. These inefficiencies are often masked, whether inadvertently or deliberately, as manufacturing is invisible to almost everyone except those who work in manufacturing. Zero waste fashion design addresses inefficiency in fabric use by reframing fabric waste as an opportunity to explore the magic of fashion; just like all fashion, zero waste fashion celebrates experimentation and the discovery of new forms.

FIGURE 1.
Dress by nothing nothing by Julian Roberts explores the innovative pattern cutting method he invented called "Subtraction Cutting." Julian Roberts.

1

TEXTILE WASTE

There are two broad categories of textile waste: waste created by industry and waste created by consumers. Preconsumer textile waste is created during the manufacture of fiber, yarn, fabric, and garments. The majority is fabric waste from garment manufacture.

Postconsumer textile waste is created by consumers and comprises garments and household textiles. This book focuses on designing out preconsumer fabric waste: zero waste fashion design.

+ FABRIC WASTE: THE NUMBERS +

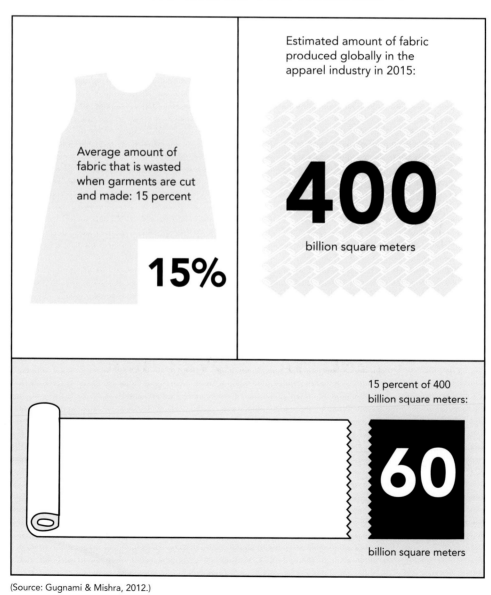

Average amount of fabric that is wasted when garments are cut and made: 15 percent

15%

Estimated amount of fabric produced globally in the apparel industry in 2015:

400

billion square meters

15 percent of 400 billion square meters:

60

billion square meters

(Source: Gugnami & Mishra, 2012.)

Fabric waste in the fashion industry is mainly treated as an economic issue. The systems that are in place ensure that the wasted fabric does not result in economic loss; however, there is evidence to show that fabric waste should also be an environmental and ethical consideration for the fashion industry (Rissanen 2013: 11–13). Fabric is a valuable and sophisticated product due to fiber extraction, spinning, design, weaving or knitting, and finishing processes. Alongside economic investment, fabric embodies investments of material, energy, water, and time. When fabric is wasted during manufacturing, these embodied investments in the wasted fabric are often lost. Textile waste recycling can recover the material investment but often requires further investments of energy, water, and time.

Zero waste fashion design in this book refers to fashion design that wastes no fabric, by integrating pattern cutting into the design process. The scope of this book is necessarily focused. A broad definition of zero waste fashion design could, for example, include garment disposal strategies as a design consideration.

The term zero waste in a fashion context emerged mainly after 2008. This has led many to think that zero waste fashion design is a new phenomenon. Working outside of fashion, Paul Palmer founded the Zero Waste Institute in the 1970s and has since published many critiques of the modern waste industry, particularly recycling. Palmer was among the first to use the term zero waste; partly due to his pioneering work, the term was more easily adapted to fashion later. Although the term zero waste fashion design is new, the practice is as old as dressing the body with skins and cloth.

This chapter introduces several historical examples of zero waste and "less waste" garments from different cultures, followed by modern examples. While it is difficult to make broad generalizations, some connections emerge. For example, it is evident that some fashion designers in the twentieth and twenty-first centuries have been influenced by cuts of historical zero waste or less waste garments. This chapter gives a snapshot of the rich diversity of zero waste garments through time and creates a solid foundation on which to inspire you to begin to experiment.

ZERO WASTE OVER TIME

Many of the historical garments covered in this chapter were not designed by a fashion designer as the role is understood today. However, we can regard all human beings as designers. In the same way that Bernard Rudofsky (1977) wrote about "architecture without architects," we can regard these garments as "zero waste fashion design without fashion designers." Many of these garments were created at times when raw materials were scarce and the processes of making yarn and fabric slow; therefore, fabrics were treated with greater respect and care, which provides a valuable lesson for designers today.

DOROTHY BURNHAM

Royal Ontario Museum

This book might not have been possible without the life work of Dorothy Burnham, a curator at the Royal Ontario Museum in Toronto. In 1973 Burnham published an exhibition catalog, "Cut My Cote," to accompany an exhibition of the same name. In the book Burnham (1973: 2) discusses the various factors affecting garment cut—the body, climate, geographic terrain, social status, and modesty—stating that they "are all important, but the material from which a garment is made is the factor that has the most influence on the particular shaping of it." Two separate developments occurred in garment cutting: those based on the shapes of animal skins and those "dependent on the rectilinear form of loom-woven cloth." Eventually these merged into one. Burnham was perhaps the first to place the efficiency of cut at the forefront of her research, uncovering the link between the loom type used for weaving by a particular culture at a particular time, the resulting fabric width, and most significantly, the relationship between fabric width, garment cut, and the resulting waste.

Zero waste in historical and traditional dress

Many fashion histories focus on Western fashion, while non-Western fashion is treated as somehow distinct and often as static over time. For zero waste fashion such an approach is inappropriate; zero waste fashion design, as defined earlier, has existed in different cultures throughout time. Examples are presented here thematically rather than chronologically, as there is no clear evolution of zero waste over time.

The first garments were animal skins draped on the body. More complex garments, such as multiple skins joined together and shaped to the body, were worn by the Plains Indians in North America, for example. With the development of woven cloth, at its simplest, a length of cloth could be worn as a garment. The himation, chiton, and peplos of ancient Greece, as well as the main piece of the sari of India, are lengths of fabric with no cutting that are draped on the body. The sari can be draped in a variety of ways, as could examples of ancient Greek dress.

To make a Japanese kimono, a narrow cloth (35–40 centimeters /13¾–15¾ inches) is woven to the required length, often 11 to 12 meters long (12–13 yards). The length is split into five lengths, and the fifth piece is split further into four pieces, for a total of eight pieces. No fabric waste is created in the cutting process. Surplus fabric in the front neck is pleated inside the collar for structure rather than cut. Similarly, the curved sleeve hem present in some kimonos is achieved by easing the excess seam allowance inside the sleeve rather than by cutting it away. A kimono is sewn by hand with a running stitch, and it is unpicked completely for washing, temporarily returning it close to its original shape as flat fabric.

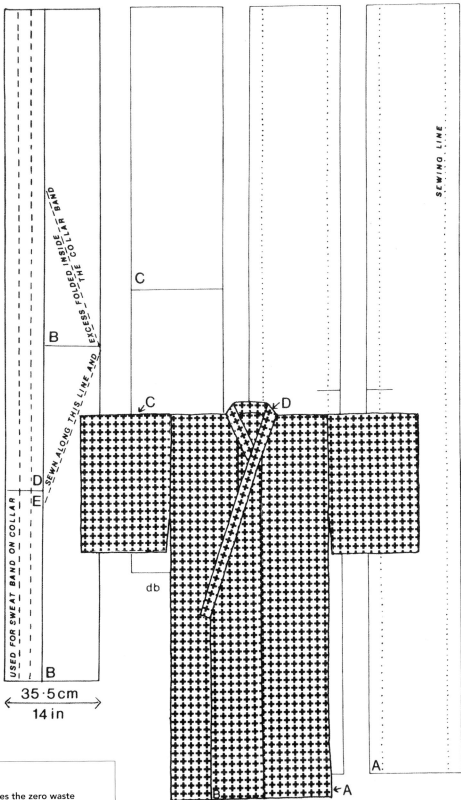

SEWING LINE

USED FOR SWEAT BAND ON COLLAR

SEWN ALONG THIS LINE AND EXCESS FOLDED INSIDE THE COLLAR BAND

35·5 cm
14 in

FIGURE 2.
The cut of this coat demonstrates the zero waste principles of cutting present in Japanese garments referred collectively to as kimono. Pattern for Man's Coat. Japanese, Early 20th century; Dorothy K. Burnham/Royal Ontario Museum.

2

Two examples of zero or less waste trousers from China (Tilke 1956) show the displacement of two large rectangles against each other, resulting in asymmetrical trousers that hang off-grain. There is no clear front or back to the pieces. In one pair, small triangular pieces are used at the waist to fit the trousers to the body. While the kimono and these trousers are made from similar shapes, the trousers demonstrate that simple geometric shapes can be joined to create dynamic forms that hang on the body in unconventional ways.

A woman's blouse from Denmark from the Middle Ages (Tilke 1956) is cut from one piece. The bodice wraps to the center back and attaches to a yoke seam from which the sleeves jut out. Burnham (1973) explains how the shape of animal skins influenced this cut. Examples of this cut can be found from various countries, for example, the Hungarian guba. A baby blouse that belonged to Timo Rissanen's grandmother (born in Finland in 1923) is based on the same cut, as are contemporary garments from Yeohlee Teng and David Telfer, as well as McQuillan and Rissanen.

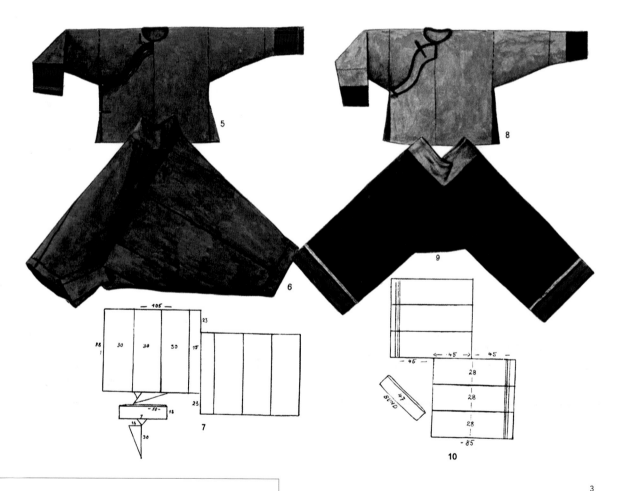

FIGURE 3.
The cuts of these trousers from China, featured by Tilke (1956), demonstrate that two rectangles can be "off-set" against each other, forcing the fabric into three-dimensional, asymmetric forms. This principle can be applied to any type of garment. Ernst Wasmuth Verlag.

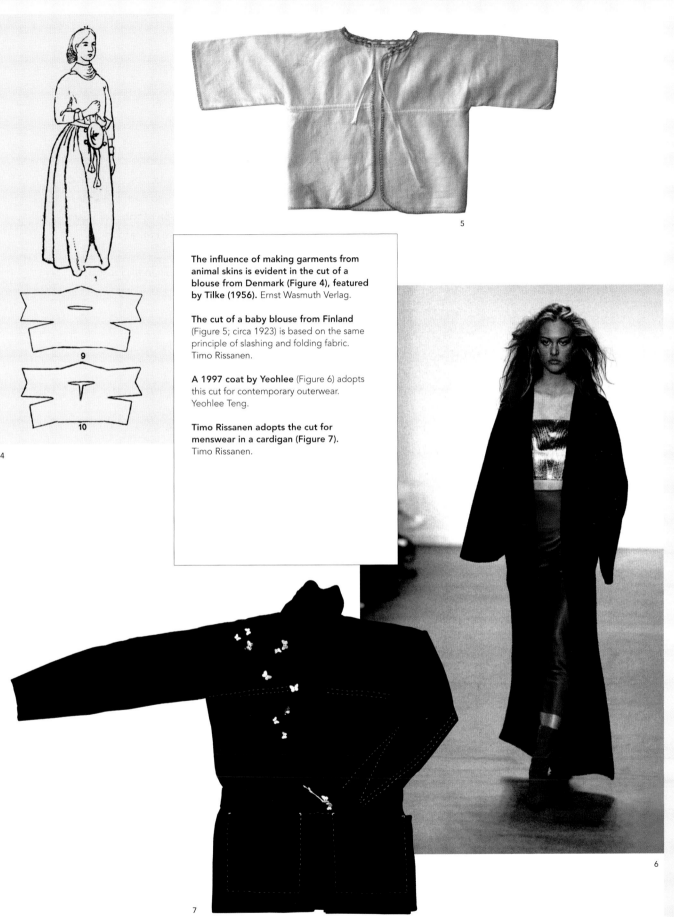

The influence of making garments from animal skins is evident in the cut of a blouse from Denmark (Figure 4), featured by Tilke (1956). Ernst Wasmuth Verlag.

The cut of a baby blouse from Finland (Figure 5; circa 1923) is based on the same principle of slashing and folding fabric. Timo Rissanen.

A 1997 coat by Yeohlee (Figure 6) adopts this cut for contemporary outerwear. Yeohlee Teng.

Timo Rissanen adopts the cut for menswear in a cardigan (Figure 7). Timo Rissanen.

4

5

6

7

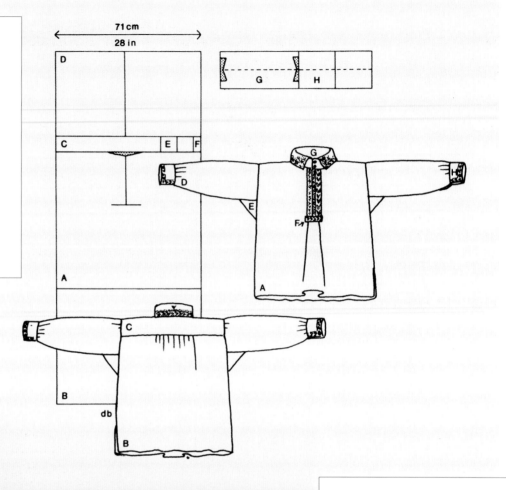

FIGURE 8.
Although the resulting garment T-shape in this shirt is similar to the Danish blouse, **the principle of cutting is different.** The shirt sleeves are cut separately through the body, and fit is refined through the use of gussets. Pattern for Man's Shirt. South American, possibly Chile; Dorothy K. Burnham/ Royal Ontario Museum.

8

FIGURE 9A.
Countless variations of historical "square-cut" shirts exist in museums, primarily from Europe and America. These began to disappear from Western dress in the nineteenth century, replaced by shirts that utilized curves around armholes and neck. This example is remarkable in that careful study has revealed that it was repaired and remodeled over a long time span of at least two, and possibly four, decades of use. Square-cut shirt (1775–1790, featured in Baumgarten et al, 1999)/The Colonial Williamsburg Foundation. Bequest of Grace Hartshorn Westerfield.

9A

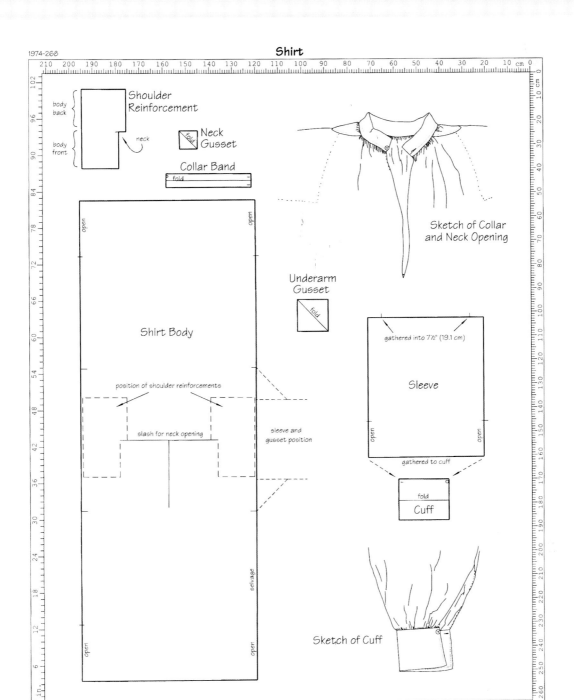

FIGURE 9B.
Study of the shirt's cut reveals that adding fabric to areas of strain, such as where the arm joins the body, can add to a garment's longevity. The opening for the neck is created with a T-shaped slash combined with gathers and a gusset.

Pattern of Colonial Williamsburg's linen shirt drafted and drawn by Linda Baumgarten and John Watson (first published in *Costume Close-Up, Clothing Construction and Pattern, 1750–1790*), used with permission. Square-cut shirt (1775–1790, featured in Baumgarten et al, 1999) Pattern/The Colonial Williamsburg Foundation. Bequest of Grace Hartshorn.

9B

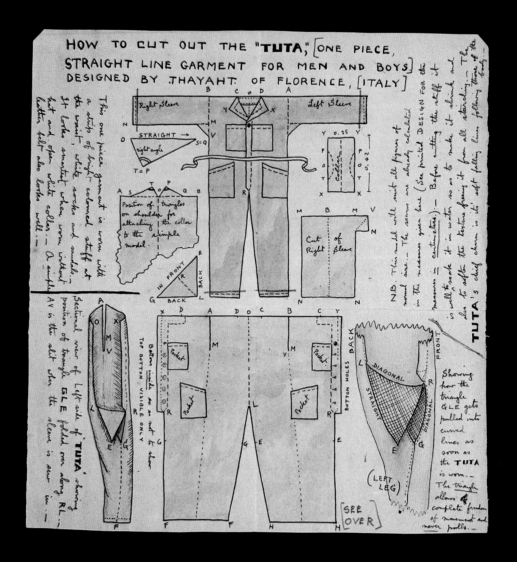

FIGURE 10.
The tuta (1919) by Thayaht (Ernesto Michahelles) is "square-cut" similar to the shirt in Figure 9. Remarkably, fit around the crotch is achieved with a triangle gusset, in contrast to the curved cut of crotch in trousers that dominates today. Private collection.

MODERN ZERO WASTE FASHION DESIGN

From early twentieth century onward, it is possible to identify the creators of zero waste and less waste garments. These demonstrate the foundation of zero waste garments, a relationship between fabric width and garment cut. While waste elimination was unlikely to be a focus for most of the creators mentioned here, it is nonetheless possible to ascertain that the garments featured here resulted in little or no fabric waste.

Zero waste moments through the twentieth century

The Italian futurist artist Thayaht (real name Ernesto Michahelles) launched the tuta, or overalls, in 1919. The body of the tuta is cut in one piece, with the cutout wedge between the legs used for front facings. Gussets under the arms and at the crotch improve fit and movement. Thayaht created several versions of the tuta, including a two-piece for men and a dress version for women.

11

FIGURE 11.
Thayaht (Ernesto Michahelles) also created versions of the tuta for women, as evident in this dress example (circa 1919). The underarm gussets are visible in the sketch. Courtesy of Radu Stern; from *Against Fashion: Clothing as Art, 1850–1930*, by Radu Stern, published by The MIT Press.

12A

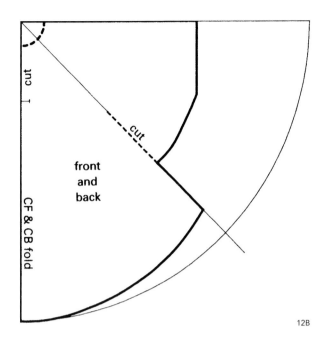

FIGURES 12A AND 12B.
This dress cut based on a full circle by Winifred Aldrich is similar to dresses and coats created by the French designer Madeleine Vionnet in the early twentieth century. The front and back fall on the straight grain, the sleeves on cross-grain, and the sides on the bias. A dress based on a half-circle would have the front hang on the straight grain, back on the cross-grain and sleeves on the bias. Winifred Aldrich and John Wiley and Sons Limited.

cut

cut

front and back

CF & CB fold

12B

Thayaht worked for Parisian couturier Madeleine Vionnet in the early 1920s. They shared an interest in dynamic symmetry: a design theory that made connections between growth rates seen in nature with proportions found in classical Greek art. Betty Kirke (1998) illustrates the patterns of several garments by Vionnet that exhibit an affinity with fabric width. For example, a dress from 1919–20 is essentially four squares of fabric, with minimal shaping. Twisting the front shoulder against the back before joining eliminates armhole and neck gape. Interestingly, Thayaht's tuta and Vionnet's square dress date from the same year: 1919. Another Vionnet dress is remarkable in that it is composed of four rectangular shapes cut on the straight grain while hanging on the bias. Cutting garments on the bias can result in more fabric waste; cutting on the straight while hanging on the bias, similar to the Chinese trousers, can help eliminate waste.

Bernard Rudofsky was a social historian who criticized the Western tradition of cutting fabric to make clothes, as to him it seemed wasteful both materially and philosophically. In 1950 he applied his knowledge of traditional dress to the Bernardo Separates range. The clothes were adjustable and one-size-fits-all, made from rectangular pieces of fabric. Rudofsky aimed to minimize waste, as well as sewing, to maintain affordability. In 1944 Rudofsky included garments by the American designer Claire McCardell as examples of zero waste fashion design in the exhibition "Are Clothes Modern?" at the Metropolitan Museum of Art in New York. During her studies at Parsons, McCardell spent a year in Paris, buying and picking apart toiles of Vionnet dresses. From these she learned Vionnet's principles of cutting, which she later applied in her designs for American mass-market production. Notably, Rudofsky also included Max Tilke's pattern diagrams in the exhibition catalog.

FIGURES 13A AND 13B.
Dress by Zandra Rhodes (1980)
demonstrates Rhodes's love and
respect for textiles. The garment
pattern is in part determined by the
geometric form of the print.
Figure 13a: San Diego History Center;
Figure 13b: Zandra Rhodes.

13A

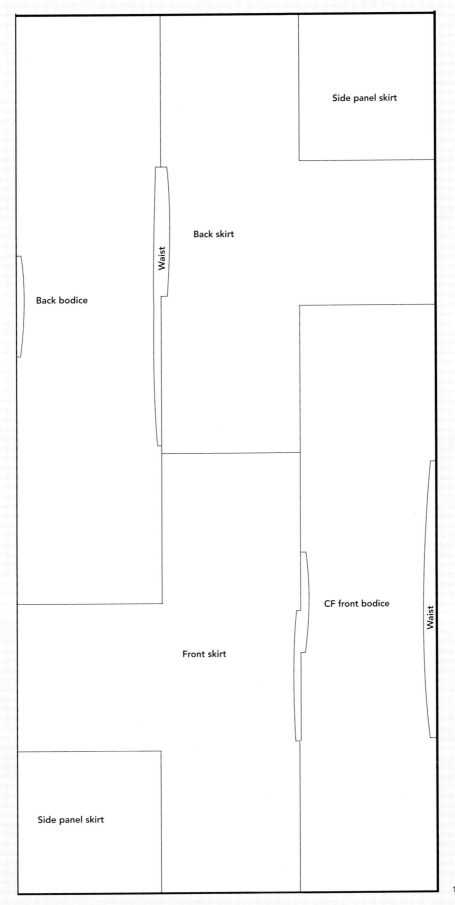

Side panel skirt

Back skirt

Waist

Back bodice

Front skirt

CF front bodice

Waist

Side panel skirt

13B

An English designer trained in the 1960s, Zandra Rhodes, often allows the printed fabric to determine the pattern shapes of a garment. Although Rhodes was trained as a textile designer, for her, pattern cutting is an integral aspect of the fashion design process. The cut of a blouse from 1979, while not entirely eliminating waste, demonstrates this approach clearly. The sleeve and peplum pieces interlock fully, while the bodice length is determined by the space left over by the aforementioned pieces. A dress from the same collection demonstrates a variation of the same textile print-drive approach to designing a garment. Tilke's book was an early influence on Rhodes,

as it had been for Rudofsky. In showing the patterns alongside drawings of garments, Tilke encouraged a different way of viewing the design of garments.

Yeohlee Teng, an American designer (see interview on pp. 193–197), has adopted fabric waste minimization as a key element of her design practice since 1981. Teng called her autumn 2009 collection "Zero Waste" to highlight her long-standing commitment to working with fabric mindfully. This was shown by having the pattern of a sarong on the runway; the model took the sarong off and placed it on the diagram.

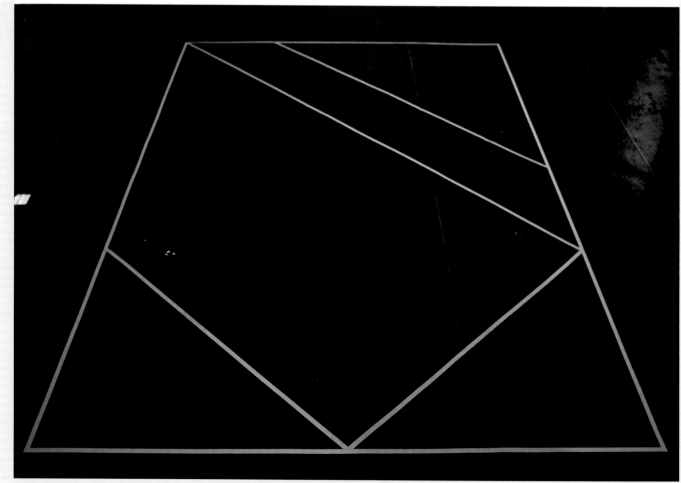

14A

14D

14E

FIGURES 14A–14E.
A sarong by Yeohlee (2009) is cut from five pieces. Remarkably, all cut lines are on the bias, demonstrating that intelligent cutting on the bias need not be wasteful. The cut was shown on the runway during the show to reiterate the importance of cut and fabric economy present in Yeohlee's work throughout her career. Yeohlee Teng.

Into the twenty-first century: gaining ground

In the first decade of the twenty-first century, zero waste fashion design has become more widely adopted worldwide. An Australian company led by Susan Dimasi and Chantal Kirby, Materialbyproduct, has produced garments without wasting fabric for over a decade. The work by Fiona Buckingham of Kyotap also warrants investigation in this respect. Another Australian, Mark Liu received considerable attention in 2007–8 for his zero waste garments. Other designers to have experimented with zero waste fashion design are Andrew Hague, whose shirt Kate Fletcher featured in her seminal book on fashion and sustainability in 2008, and Friederike von Wedel-Parlow, who has established the master's degree on fashion and sustainability at Esmod Berlin.

FIGURE 15.
Dress, trousers, and top by Holly McQuillan; digital print by Genevieve Packer (2011). This ensemble from the exhibition "Yield" demonstrates Holly McQuillan's use of "embedded zero waste" where multiple garments are developed in a single zero waste pattern. Holly McQuillan; Photograph by Thomas McQuillan.

15

FIGURE 16.
Timo Rissanen created this zero waste coat and leggings during his PhD research (2008). Timo Rissanen; Photograph by Thomas McQuillan.

CHAPTER 1

FIGURE 17.
Dress by Study NY by Tara St James (2010). The Four Ways Dress by Tara St James can be worn multiple ways through the fastening of buttons. She has re-released this piece many times since it was first designed, demonstrating its versitility. Tara St James; Photograph by Thomas McQuillan.

FIGURE 18.
Dress by Caroline Priebe (2009). This simple garment illustrates how zero waste design need not be complex to be contemporary. Caroline Priebe; Photograph by Thomas McQuillan.

18

19

FIGURE 19.
Jacket by Samuel Formo (2010).
Alongside leaders in architecture
and product design, Samuel Formo's
zero waste jacket earned him the place
as a finalist in *Metropolis* magazine's
2009 Next Generation Design
Competition, and he was a finalist in
the Fashioning the Future competition.
Samuel Formo; Photograph by Thomas
McQuillan.

FIGURE 20.
Three-piece suit by Jennifer Whitty
(2011). Jennifer Whitty's three-piece suit is
informed by the contrast between Western
and Eastern approaches to clothing,
Wabi-sabi, symbols of eternity, embracing
mistakes, and the dualities of order and
disorder, and spontaneity and control.
Jennifer Whitty; Photograph by Thomas
McQuillan.

20

FIGURE 21.
Shirt and jacket by Julia Lumsden
(2010). Julian Lumsden's shirt and
jacket were both created through
the use of CAD sofware (Accumark)
and explore traditions of menswear
in zero waste fashion context.
Julia Lumsden; Photograph by
Thomas McQuillan.

21

22

FIGURE 22.
Dress by Carla Fernandez (2008). Unlike the pattern-cutting taught in the Western (European) tradition, indigenous clothes are often constructed from large geometric shapes. Fernandez uses these traditional forms as the conceptual basis for Taller Flora garments, while collaborating with rural communities to create the label's fabrics and garments. The cloths are often woven with traditional back-strapped looms; these are handcrafted into carefully considered garments that celebrate not only the cloth but the culture and wisdom from which it originates. Carla Fernandez; Photograph by Thomas McQuillan.

FIGURE 23.
Coat by David Telfer (2010). This coat by David Telfer incorporates principles found in clothing from various cultures around the world. The sleeves wrap over the shoulders from the front to the back, while the back wraps at the sides to the front. The malleability of the cloth means that a somewhat rigid-appearing geometric cut takes its three-dimensional shape from the body within the garment. David Telfer; Photograph by Thomas McQuillan.

23

Most of the authors' zero waste fashion design practice has occurred within academia. Rissanen commenced his PhD study on zero waste fashion design in 2004, and he started blogging about it in 2006. McQuillan completed a master's degree in 2005; zero waste fashion design was integral to it. McQuillan discovered Rissanen online in 2008, and they have been exchanging ideas ever since. In 2011 McQuillan and Rissanen curated and exhibited in Yield, a survey exhibition of zero waste fashion design. Included in Yield were Rhodes, Teng, Alabama Chanin, Julian Roberts, Carla Fernandez, Julia Lumsden, Jennifer Whitty, David Telfer, Tara St James of Study NY, Caroline Priebe of Uluru, and Samuel Formo. St James presented her first collection for Study NY, entirely zero waste, in September 2009. The collection was based on squares: look 1 in the show was made from one square, look 2 from two, and so forth. St James has included zero waste garments in each collection since. Priebe's Westlake dress and its pattern were also exhibited in "Ethics + Aesthetics = Sustainable Fashion" in 2009, curated by Sarah Scaturro and Francesca Granata. In spring 2011, Priebe taught the zero waste course at Parsons. Sam Formo created a zero waste jacket during his studies at California College of the Arts (CCA). It must be noted that Andrew Hague, Caroline Priebe, and Samuel Formo are all former students of Lynda Grose, professor at CCA and a fashion industry sustainability pioneer.

McQuillan's colleagues and students at Massey University have experimented with zero waste fashion design extensively, most notably her colleague Jennifer Whitty and former student Julia Lumsden (see interview on pp.144–147). Lumsden's collection included several zero waste men's shirts.

Carla Fernandez is a Mexican designer whose design practice draws from her research into indigenous textiles and dress, noting that fragmenting the fabric and losing some of it makes the story told by a piece of cloth incomplete. She collaborates with indigenous artisans, who weave the fabrics for her. The cuts of indigenous garments inform her garments. The approach by Fernandez, of applying the wisdom of countless generations to contemporary garments, follows that of Rudofsky five decades earlier.

David Telfer, a British designer, has explored zero waste fashion design alongside other concerns for efficiency, such as minimal fabric utilization and minimal seaming. The cut of the duffel coat he exhibited in Yield bears a resemblance to the blouses discussed earlier. The body, sleeves, and hood are not separated from the original piece as slashes are used.

An increasing number of students around the world are experimenting with zero waste fashion design. Rissanen and McQuillan have taught zero waste fashion design at Parsons and Massey University, respectively, for several years, and other schools, such as Lahti University of Applied Sciences in Finland, have incorporated zero waste fashion design into the curriculum for some time. Simone Austen's entirely zero waste undergraduate collection demands acknowledgment, as does a collection by Yitzhak Abecassis, who created a collection entirely through cutting slashes into single pieces of fabric. Similarly, Laura Poole's undergraduate collection was entirely zero waste. For zero waste fashion design to be more broadly adopted, it needs to be incorporated into fashion education globally, as education provides the ideal environment without the economic and time constraints of industry.

The aims of this book are to demystify the process of zero waste fashion design and to encourage more companies, educators, and students to experiment with it. The examples so far demonstrate that this is not only possible, but it is also happening.

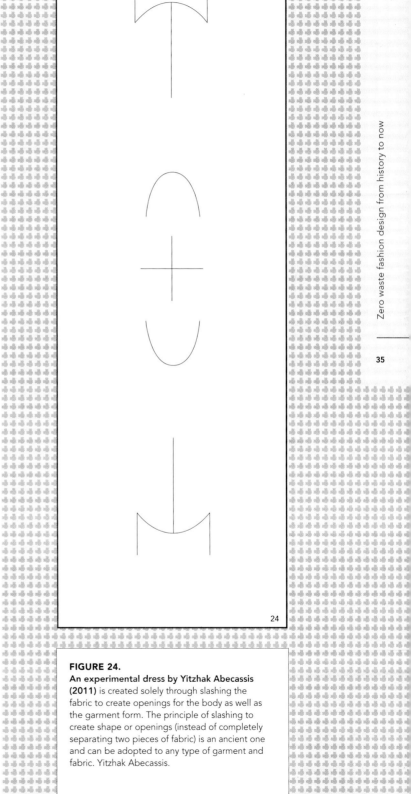

24

FIGURE 24.
An experimental dress by Yitzhak Abecassis
(2011) is created solely through slashing the
fabric to create openings for the body as well as
the garment form. The principle of slashing to
create shape or openings (instead of completely
separating two pieces of fabric) is an ancient one
and can be adopted to any type of garment and
fabric. Yitzhak Abecassis.

Collar

Back

Front

Front

25

FIGURE 25.
A coat by Simone Austen (2011)
uses slashes to cut the sleeves in one
with the body. Simone Austen.

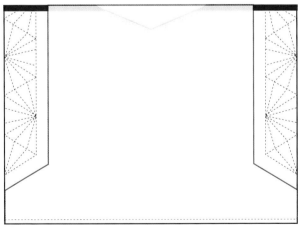

26

FIGURE 26.
Laura Poole's entire graduation collection (2010, University of Technology Sydney) was zero waste. In this top the piece removed to create the neck is developed into applique through decorative embroidery. Laura Poole.

27

FIGURE 27.
The top and skirt by Maja Stabel
(see interview on pp. 39–40)
(2013) take advantage of a soft
fabric, allowing a fluid form
with rectangular pattern pieces.
Maja Stabel.

INTERVIEW WITH MAJA STABEL

Maja Stabel is a Norwegian fashion designer and illustrator. After a zero waste project for Danish designer David Andersen, Stabel set up her own brand focusing on zero waste, and has designed for the Norwegian brand Age of Enlightenment, which focuses on sustainability in fashion.

Visit Maja's website here: www.majastabel.com

+ **How did you come to design zero waste garments?**

During my fashion design studies, I started to question being just another designer and making more clothes, which we really don't need; so I asked, what if I could use fashion to do good?

After I finished my bachelor's degree I started on sustainable fashion design studies in Copenhagen. I came up with doing zero waste design in my head before ever reading about it. I was like, "of course!" I will use the whole fabric piece in my design, which is a great new concept as well! Shortly thereafter I read about it and realized that several designers were already practicing it. I didn't research to see how others did it; so I just figured out my own way of doing zero waste design by making triangles, and later rectangles, to make it easier in production.

My story in short is that I made a zero waste assignment at school, an imaginary collection for Danish designer David Andersen. He came to the presentation and loved it and asked me to design a collection for him, which I did. While working for him, his investor noticed me and loved my zero waste concept. He wanted to start up a new brand with me as the designer, and it lasted three months before he realized millions aren't made overnight. I wanted to stay true to my vision, and we parted ways, as I took the collection I had made and moved home to do it all myself.

This is how Stabel came to be. Starting up on your own isn't a walk in the park, so to be able to continue on this path, I am now designing zero waste for a new Norwegian sustainable brand called Age of Enlightenment (www.aoeclothing.com).

+ Have there been any positive surprises about designing zero waste garments? What have been some of the larger challenges with designing zero waste garments, and how have you tackled them?

I love designing zero waste because there is always a challenge in making the math to fit and get the proportions right, and this is where the interesting design solutions come in. This is where I get creative, and when I get everything to add up, it's an exhilarating feeling!

+ Zero waste was integral to the Stabel brand. Did you share this with your customers, and how did they respond?

Yes, I absolutely shared it with my customers, and they loved the concept! As I made all my patterns with only rectangles, they were amazed by the puzzle I made and that it also could be made into a design garment. The thing was that this concept fitted very well with the clean Scandinavian design aesthetics, and my customers loved that they got "two in one"— design and sustainability.

+ What opportunities do you see for zero waste fashion design becoming more widely adopted in industry?

I would love to see more zero waste in the industry, and I have tried to make a concept which is really easy (all the patterns are made up of only rectangles)—both for the customers to understand and the factories to make. I am all about "sharing is caring," and I'm thinking about making my designs more available and maybe accessible for others to make. We are talking about doing this through Age of Enlightenment—sharing designs in the same way that Tesla is sharing their patents. I'm also thinking about making DIY kits with zero waste garments—puzzles with only rectangles to put together, something that is easy and everyone can understand. I think this is the only way forward—to share and collaborate with others—and I also think this could help to make zero waste more widely adopted in the industry.

SHORT CUTS

1 Sometimes when we look at a historical garment, we overlook the context in which they were made and worn. Can you identify any social, economic, or technological changes that may have impacted on the prevalence of zero waste fashion design practices over time?

2 Why might zero waste fashion design be experiencing a resurgence at this point in time?

3 Speculate on possible opportunities and barriers for zero waste fashion design, in your own practice, within the curriculum of your school, and at the level of industry.

pattern cutting as a fashion design tool

Pattern cutting in zero waste fashion design is a highly creative activity: it is fashion design. Design ideas are generated, rather than reacted to, during this type of pattern cutting. This chapter frames creative pattern cutting as one of the foundations of zero waste fashion design. Expert cutters from around the world demonstrate that pattern cutting can be explorative, even fun. Where conventional design processes often conclude in the pattern, zero waste fashion design can begin with it.

FASHION DESIGN AND PATTERN CUTTING

Pattern cutting is traditionally written about and taught as a specialist technique, performed by someone in a discrete role. It is treated as distinct from fashion design, and often pattern cutters are not involved in the design of the garment. They may not even be in the same location as the designer, placing constraints on collaboration. While the pattern cutter might have some sense of the amount of fabric waste that a single garment creates, she/he usually does not see the amount of waste created in the factory. The fashion designer is unlikely to even see the waste created by the sample garment.

In contrast to this dominant hierarchy of roles, pattern cutting is integral to zero waste fashion design. Pattern cutting in zero waste fashion design is a generative rather than a reactive activity. Most pattern cutting responds to a sketch or an idea expressed another way (Rissanen 2007). In zero waste fashion design, this can occur but does not always; pattern cutting can be the activity that generates the idea. For zero waste fashion design to work, pattern cutting must be a dynamic, creative, generative, and open-ended practice. The traditional separation of the fashion design and pattern cutting roles, particularly in larger mass-market and ready-to-wear companies, is a key challenge for zero waste fashion design and further distances fashion design from issues it could address, such as fabric waste.

CONVENTIONAL FASHION DESIGN AND FASHION MANUFACTURE HIERARCHIES

FASHION DESIGN

Fashion designer

Pattern cutter

Sample cutter

Sample machinist

FASHION MANUFACTURE

Fashion designer

Pattern cutter

Pattern grader

Marker planner & maker

Cutter

Machinist

FIGURE 28.
The conventional organization of roles within the fashion industry is a linear hierarchy. Feedback upwards in the hierarchy is possible but when the pattern cutter is in a different country from the designer, true collaboration is difficult. Holly McQuillan; Timo Rissanen.

ZERO-WASTE FASHION DESIGN
AND FASHION MANUFACTURE ORGANIZATION

FASHION DESIGN AND MANUFACTURE

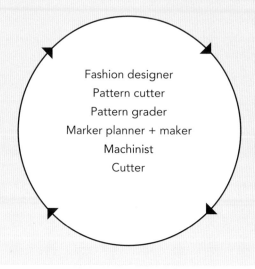

Fashion designer
Pattern cutter
Pattern grader
Marker planner + maker
Machinist
Cutter

29

FIGURE 29.
A nonhierarchical organization of roles is preferable in zero waste fashion design, and allows a fluid interplay between all the components that make a successful design. Holly McQuillan; Timo Rissanen.

To date this arrangement of roles has received somewhat limited interest from researchers, including those focused on zero waste fashion design. If one of the keys to eliminating fabric waste lies in the rethinking of how the roles of fashion designer and pattern cutter interact in particular, then the potential impediments to this rethinking, and possible solutions to these impediments, must be considered.

This also impacts how we think about fashion design education. Historically the focus of fashion design education has been to teach sketching and drawing skills as "design" and pattern cutting and sewing skills as either somewhat separate from design or subservient to it. There is no doubt about the technical acumen offered in most pattern cutting books aimed at fashion design students. The issue with many of them, however, is that pattern cutting is usually presented as a rigid technical process. As a consequence fashion design students tend to regard and approach pattern cutting as a "closed" activity rather than an open-ended process of discovery and thinking.

The roles of fashion designer and pattern cutter are divided and specialized to achieve higher productivity. This can lead to obstacles and missed opportunities for solving issues related to sustainability, such as fabric waste, which often require a holistic approach. Reconfiguring the roles within the fashion design system, and dismantling some of the hierarchical relationships, will likely require greater integration of the many design roles within, led from education and industry. It would be worth investigating what unexpected benefits, if any, these new, nonhierarchical ways of interacting might bring about.

CREATIVE PATTERN CUTTING

Creative pattern cutting in fashion design is not new. Some historical fashion designers, such as Madeleine Vionnet, Cristóbal Balenciaga, and Charles James, designed through cutting, by draping fabric on the figure. Kirke (1998) tells a detailed story of Vionnet's training, which she began as a seamstress at the age of twelve. Balenciaga was trained as a tailor (Rennolds Milbank 1985). With each designer it is easy to see how technical expertise fed creative thinking, and in turn how creativity drove technical execution, often bringing about new ways of cutting and constructing garments. This section reviews some contemporary researchers and practitioners, aiming to demonstrate the diversity of approaches.

30

FIGURE 30.
Jonathan KYLE Farmer's approach in his Drawing with Scissors project (2013) is in equal parts fashion design and pattern cutting. He "draws" by cutting paper into clothed figures, a form of spontaneous pattern cutting. Jonathan KYLE Farmer.

FIGURE 31A.
Timo Rissanen (2011) designed
and made these pajamas from
his grandmother's bedsheets
dating to the 1940s. He made it a
requirement for himself that all of
the fabric needed to be used.
Timo Rissanen; Photograph by
Mariano Garcia.

31A

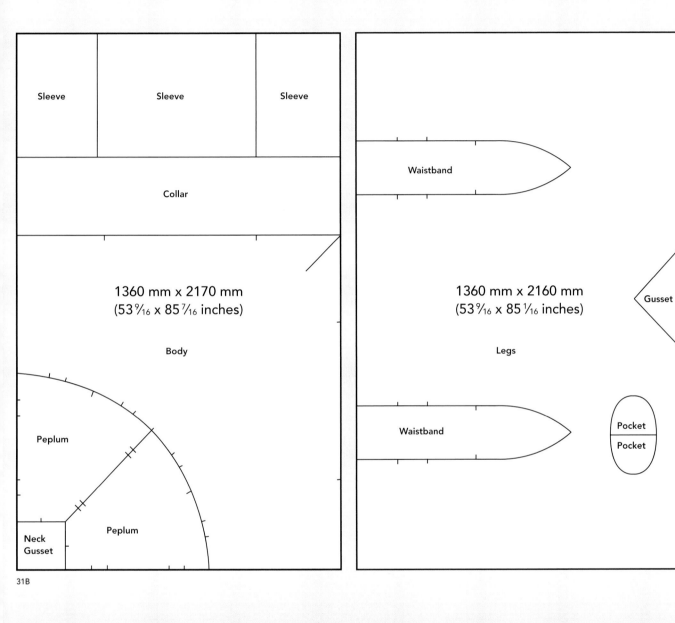

Sleeve

Sleeve

Sleeve

Collar

1360 mm x 2170 mm
(53 9/16 x 85 7/16 inches)

Body

Peplum

Peplum

Neck
Gusset

Waistband

1360 mm x 2160 mm
(53 9/16 x 85 1/16 inches)

Legs

Gusset

Waistband

Pocket

Pocket

31B

FIGURE 31B.
The body of the pajama top is based on a quarter circle, with center back on bias, and fronts on straight and cross grains. The cut of the trouser is based on a sketch by Julian Roberts, with gusset borrowed from Thayaht. Timo Rissanen.

From the 1970s, Issey Miyake, Rei Kawakubo of Comme des Garcons, and Yohji Yamamoto and other Japanese designers have led the fashion world with fashion underpinned by creative cutting. In their work they have repeatedly challenged many Western pattern cutting conventions. Since 2005 Nakamichi has begun to challenge the traditions of pattern cutting literature through the *Pattern Magic* book series.

In 2013 Dr. Kevin Almond convened a conference, titled Creative Cut, on creative pattern cutting. The conference built on an earlier paper by Almond (2010) on the same topic. This was perhaps the first international congregation of scholars who largely agreed that pattern cutting could be a creative activity, as well as the subject of academic research. For a field to develop and expand, it needs nourishment through rigorous inquiry. Pattern cutting research has been pioneered by Dr. Winifred Aldrich (see interview on pp. 49–50), beautifully summed up in the two editions (Aldrich 1996; Aldrich 2007) of *Fabric, Form, and Flat Pattern Cutting*, and *Fabrics and Pattern Cutting* (Aldrich 2012).

32

FIGURE 32.
Calico toiles of garments by Keri Cowdell (left), and Rachel Vickers (right), 2009, students at University of Huddersfield. The creative potential of pattern cutting is emphasized at the university and harnessed by the students, as evident here. Photograph by Kevin Almond.

INTERVIEW WITH WINIFRED ALDRICH

Winifred Aldrich, an English designer and academic, is perhaps the most published author on pattern cutting. The first edition of her *Metric Pattern Cutting* was published in 1980. Aldrich was an early proponent of sustainability concerns in textiles: a section of her 1996 book *Fabrics and Flat Pattern Cutting* discussed the ecological issues of fibres.

+ **You have always connected fashion design and pattern cutting in your texts. How do you see the relationship between fashion design and pattern cutting?**

My work and interests as an industrial designer, teacher, and researcher have always required an intimate relationship between fashion design and pattern cutting. It is particularly in the field of mass production that I can offer a point of view. The restrictions of cost, retail demands, fabric developments, and production possibilities present challenges that require the designer to have pattern cutting skills and a flexible approach to new ideas. Pattern cutting for mass production requires the designer to bring to the company experimental cut and to extend the range of pattern cutting knowledge and skills. Pattern cutting that is placed entirely with pattern or CAD technologists can become reduced to pattern modification and the recycling of past ideas. Fashion design operates in a broader field, from the designer working in a small workshop, to the world of couture with great resources. It is from these areas that most new philosophies of fashion design arise, which respond to artistic, cultural, or social influences. These ideas can revolutionize change and impact mass clothing production. However, other influences can be in competition when faced with costs or shortages of resources.

+ **You have been concerned with environmental issues from early on. How did this become an interest for you?**

Fabric plays a major part in realizing the cut of a garment. When researching into the fabric qualities that make significant changes to the shape and drape of a design, I became aware of the complex fabric technology that that many fabrics required. This was particularly so in the case of many basic garments used in mass production. This complexity covered the fibers, blends, and finishes. The use of these fabrics creates a dilemma for designers concerned with ecology. The market trend for continual change and "throw away fashion" increases the problem.

+ We regard you as a pioneer in the scholarship about fashion design and pattern cutting. What are your thoughts on zero waste fashion design?

The depletion of natural resources (and the human tragedies that have occurred through global warming) is at last being realized. However, the desire of the market for ever-increasing production provides a barrier that only a change in design philosophy toward sustainable fashion design can overcome. As fabric is usually the greatest cost to a manufacturer and to the environment, there could be less use of fabrics needing complex technology. With regard to design for mass production and the reduction of waste, account has to be taken of sizing and the total amount of fabric it takes to make the garment. The public have to desire change and be able to make choices. A new design philosophy has to be adopted by the majority of the population. The reduction in information on labeling makes this difficult. Many internet sites list only "textile" on garments. The designer now has a responsibility as an educator and as a means of affecting change.

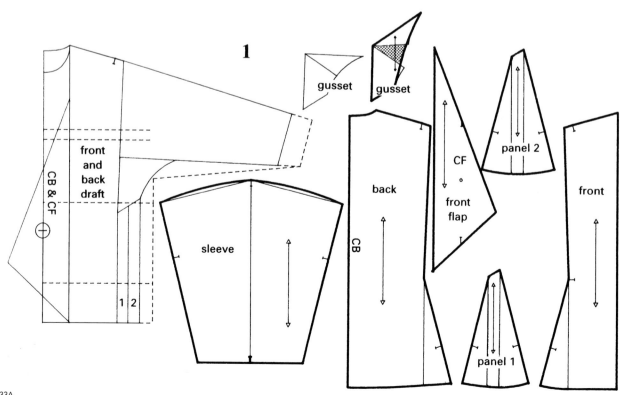

FIGURES 33A AND 33B.
Although not zero waste, this jacket by **Winifred Aldrich** could be adopted for zero waste somewhat easily due to its use of a limited number of angles to create the form. Winifred Aldrich; John Wiley and Sons Limited.

33B

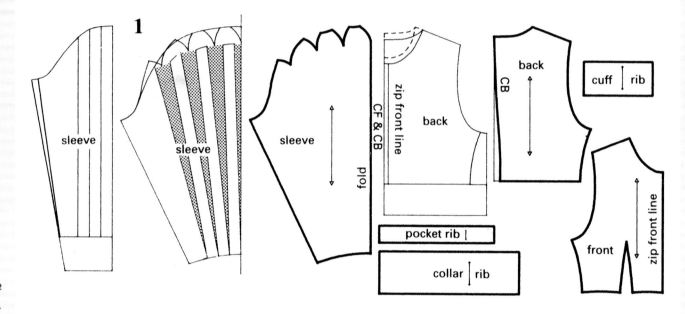

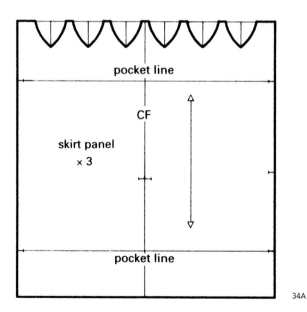

34B

FIGURES 34A AND 34B.
This coat by Winifred Aldrich could be adopted for
zero waste in countless different ways. For example,
pieces of fully fashioned (knitted to shape) rib could be
used to create some of the shaping, replacing some of
the curved lines. The skirt panel and the pocket opening
could be redesigned as the negative space of the
sleeve. Constantly looking at patterns for their design
potential is an essential part of zero waste fashion
design. Winifred Aldrich; John Wiley and Sons Limited.

INTERVIEW WITH RICKARD LINDQVIST

Rickard Lindqvist is a Swedish fashion designer and pattern cutter with a PhD from The Swedish School of Textiles. His PhD was a critical examination of the foundations that the dominant pattern cutting methods in fashion design are built upon. Through his practice-based research he has proposed an alternative approach that has the living, moving body as its kinetic foundation. Lindqvist was trained as a tailor and worked for Vivienne Westwood, both experiences building toward the fundamentals of his research.

Visit Richard's website here: www.rickardlindqvist.com

+ How would you describe the relationship between fashion design and pattern cutting?

Pattern cutting is one of the activities that constitute fashion design. From a making perspective, I suppose we are dealing with the parameters of shape, material, and color, while creating dress; then pattern cutting is for many types of garments the activity that addresses shape. In the various industrial, educational, and artisanal environments I have been working in, pattern cutting has always had as vital a role in the design process as the development of materials and colors.

In the industry I believe that pattern cutting is occasionally taken for granted as a service provided by the manufacturer or a subcontractor and not something controlled by the initiator or the designing part of the process. I believe this has come to be partly due to the commercial demands for a confirmative shape in contemporary garments, which further may be related to today's universal usage of the dominant tailoring matrix, further addressed below.

FIGURE 35.
Dominant approximation of the body for pattern cutting, the tailoring matrix, by Rickard Lindqvist.
Rickard Lindqvist's PhD explored an alternative to the dominant matrix used in tailoring. Here you see the matrix used to generate the majority of tailored garments. Rickard Lindqvist.

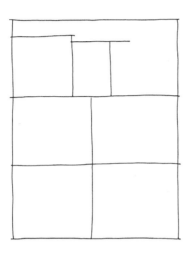

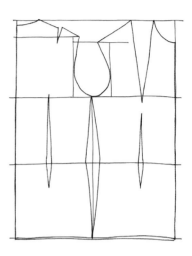

35

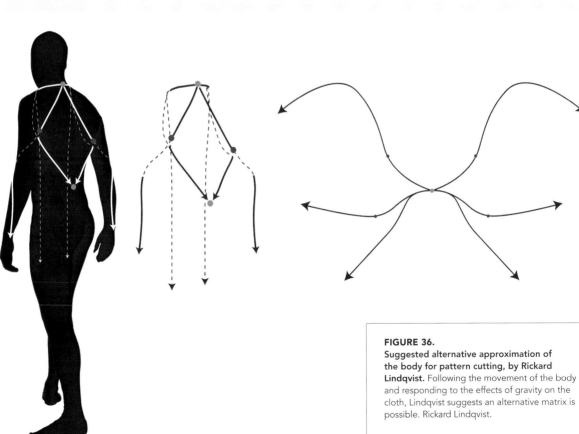

FIGURE 36.
Suggested alternative approximation of the body for pattern cutting, by Rickard Lindqvist. Following the movement of the body and responding to the effects of gravity on the cloth, Lindqvist suggests an alternative matrix is possible. Rickard Lindqvist.

36

+ How would you describe what you've done so far—is it replacing/adding to/improving a system of pattern cutting/ making blocks/something else?

I am developing an alternative theory (system) for pattern cutting that is derived from the actual moving body in interaction with the fabric dressing it. This is to be seen in comparison with the prevalent system of pattern cutting that was developed from measurements of a static body in an upright position. The main knowledge contribution is hence an alternative approximation of the body visualized through a number of direction lines and key biomechanical points on the body.

The theory has been developed through concrete experimentation (draping and cutting into fabric on a live model). From these experiments an initial hypothesis was set up. This was then followed by the making of a number of design examples with the purpose to further develop and enhance the theory while at the same validate it (i.e., demonstrate that functional and expressional garments may be created by utilizing it as the foundation for cutting).

The main aim for this work has been an insight that the vertical and horizontal guidelines used in the prevalent discourse of pattern cutting have very little to do with the actual body and the fabric that dresses it. The point of developing a new theory and to challenge the dominant one is to present alternative propositions and foundations for the design practice, which hopefully may lead to new functions and expressions in dress.

So far the theory has mainly been displayed as guidelines for draping practices and for creating a general understanding of the moving body in interaction with garments. Further possible development (research) areas for it may, for example, be in developing new types of grading principles, developing new kinds of flat construction principles, developing manufacturing setups, etc.

+ In "On the Logic of Pattern Cutting," you write that using patterns as a design tool can "end up being about funny patterns" and not "the expression of the body." However, isn't "the expression of the body" a subjective notion? Whose body? What expression? What about the expression of the cloth? Some zero waste designers work with rectangular shapes because "abstracting the body in fabric can in fact give the body expression." What are your thoughts on the relationship between the body, cloth, and garment design?

This might be unclearly stated. What I sometimes find problematic is when designers focus on their pattern cutting techniques to such an extent that what arguably ought to be their main focus, the body and its relation to the garment (an extended expression of the body), is given less attention. This is regardless of the shape of the parts constituting the garments or with the volume or tightness of a garment. Instead this addresses where to focus one's decisive vision and judgment in the design process. I have at times experienced, when students and fellow designers have been focused and excited about a technical concept to such an extent that they consider their work done and successful when the aim of this concept has been achieved, that the relation between artifact and body has then been overlooked.

+ **Your innovative and very much three-dimensional way of viewing the dressing of bodies has much to offer the field of zero waste fashion. How might your approach support the work of someone wanting to explore a zero waste way of dressing the body?**

Regardless of how one relates and chooses to deal with the waste in the fashion industry I do hope that the outcomes of my research will help designers with a better understanding of the interaction between body and garments. What I do is primarily not about cutting garments out of one single piece of fabric, as is shown in my diagrams, but instead proposing an alternative theoretical framework for pattern cutting. The one-piece patterns are to be seen as "beautiful proofs" of clear equations clarifying a design problem.

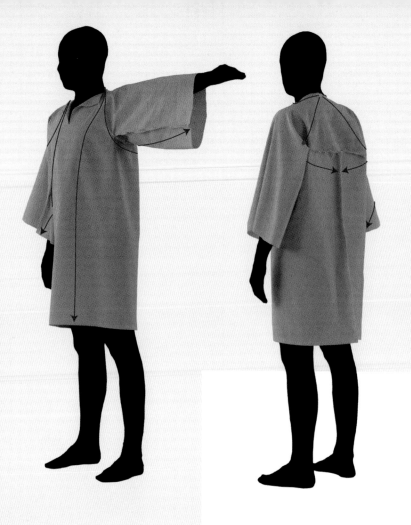

FIGURE 37.
Suggested alternative
approximation applied on
rectangular cut garment,
by Rickard Lindqvist. This
simple rectangular cut garment
demonstrated a simple
application of the alternative
matrix. This pattern could also
easily be made zero waste.
Rickard Lindqvist.

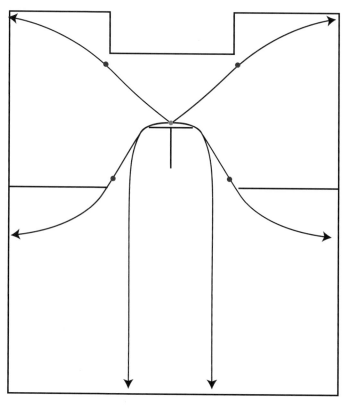

37

38

FIGURE 38.
Suggested alternative approximation applied on shell jacket pattern, by Rickard Lindqvist. Lindqvist's one piece Shell Jacket pattern and design demonstrates that unconventional patterns can lead to conventional forms—an approach that can be useful for zero waste fashion design. Rickard Lindqvist.

CREATIVE PATTERN CUTTERS FROM AROUND THE WORLD

The Swedish fashion designer and researcher Rickard Lindqvist (see interview on pp. 54–57) (2013) identifies that the standard tailor's matrix is what both flat pattern and drape pattern approaches are built from in Western dress. Most assumptions about garment patterns and their relationship to the body are formed on this foundation. He argues that there is no inherent truth to this system and that it has few "connections to the biodynamics of the body and its relation to the fabric" (Lindqvist, personal correspondence 2014).

Lindquist's (2013) study, "On the Logic of Pattern Cutting," builds on ancient wrapping approaches to dressing the body and further explores the work of Genevieve Sevin-Doering. According to Sevin-Doering it makes no sense to split the body at side seams or shoulders (cited in Lindqvist; originally from Sevin-Doering 2007). Lindqvist's work explores the body and its movement and applies this understanding to the drafting of patterns in ways that the standard tailor's block pattern does not, proposing an alternative model in order to open up for new expressions and functions in dress. The standard tailor's grid, or matrix, is reimagined as lines falling down and flowing around the body. This is combined with pivot points and moments of movement and tension, such as the nape of the neck, front and back elbow, front and back knee, front armhole, neck/shoulder intersection, or back waist and buttocks.

It is worth noting that Lindqvist's matrix was developed for menswear and may possibly require additional points for womenswear, at the bust area for instance. The overall process results in a body-led design process that, while it does not result in zero waste garments (indeed fabric use is not necessarily considered at all), provides valuable ways of seeing the relationship between garment, pattern, and body form in new ways.

Shingo Sato is a Japanese designer and fashion design educator known for Transformational Reconstruction, a pattern and garment design process that combines sketching with pattern cutting on the dress form. In one of his approaches, Sato makes a toile of a basic block, which he places on a dress form and then draws style lines on it. He then cuts the muslin up along the style lines, and transfers the resulting flat pieces to paper patterns. As Fasanella (2010) points out, this is somewhat straightforward dart manipulation for an experienced pattern cutter. However, for a novice, such as a fashion student, this can be a highly effective way of learning how to innovate with garment form through seaming. Testament to this is Sato's schedule of workshops in fashion schools around the world.

FIGURE 39.
Shingo Sato working on a
Transformation Reconstruction garment.
Sato's work explores achieving silhouettes
utilizing complex seam placement.
Shingo Sato.

FIGURE 40.
Transformation Reconstruction garment
by Shingo Sato. A creative approach to
pattern cutting is crucial to zero waste
fashion design in order to eliminate fabric
waste while creating a beautiful garment.
Learning from creative pattern cutters
like Sato is essential in achieving that.
Shingo Sato.

Greg Climer is an American designer and design educator with a focus on creative cutting. Since 2013 at Parsons in New York, he has taught a course, titled Creative Construction, which he built upon his research into creative pattern cutting and construction practices. Developing the course arose from Climer recognizing that conventional approaches to teaching pattern cutting often led to design work that was at best "known." For example, manipulating or eliminating darts, or transferring them to seams, is often done in somewhat rote ways by students.

Climer (2013) takes the students' own bodies as teaching tools. He pairs students up and has them make plaster casts of each others' faces. The students draw lines alongside the "valleys and mountains" of the resulting mask until all have been traced. The mask is cut up until it lays flat. The result is a pattern of the student's face, with darts and seams creating the indents and protrusions of the brow, nose, and mouth. Like Sato's approach, Climer's exercise opens students to thinking about the design potential of seams and darts effectively and quickly.

FIGURE 41.
Face pattern taped together by Greg Climer.
Taping the two-dimensional pattern into a three-dimensional form is a fast yet lasting learning experience for students on principles that underpin all pattern cutting. Greg Climer.

41

42

FIGURE 42.
Flat pattern for a face by Greg Climer.
This exercise is effective in getting students
to understand how seams and darts create
form. Greg Climer.

Julian Roberts is an English fashion designer
and educator with an undergraduate degree
in womenswear and a master's degree in
menswear. He is the inventor of a pattern
cutting technique called Subtraction Cutting.
He has shown thirteen collections at London
Fashion Week that utilized this technique and
currently teaches the technique globally. He
credits the difficulty he had with understanding
conventional pattern cutting, in combination
with a love of cloth and geometry, with driving
him to invent his own way of dressing the
body. In Subtraction Cutting, the patterns
are not cut to represent the outward shape;
instead they represent the negative spaces
within the garment. The results are garments
constructed from huge sheets of cloth, with
unusual shaped holes that the body passes
through. This approach incorporates adventure,
chance discovery, and the ability to cut fast and
inaccurately without using complex numerical
mathematics. His approach offers many
opportunities for those wishing to explore zero
waste fashion design, particularly through the
elimination of the way conventional garment
patterns divide the body (front/back, darts,
shoulder/side seams) and the implementation of
techniques, such as "The Plug," which enables
any shape to plug any hole so long as the seam
length is the same.

FIGURE 43.
Pattern cutting process of dress designed through the "Plug" technique by Julian Roberts. A triangle is "plugged" into a shaped hole. Julian Roberts.

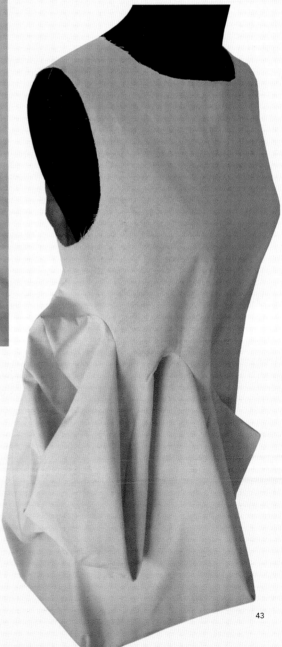

43

FIGURE 44.
"Plug" and "Displacement" techniques explained by Roberts during a workshop. Julian Roberts.

44

45

FIGURE 45.
Five variations of subtraction cutting in Julian Roberts' studio, 2014. In between teaching Subtraction Cutting workshops around the world Roberts returns to his studio to reflect and put into practice what he learns during the workshops, reminding us that pattern cutting and fashion design are continuous learning processes. Julian Roberts.

For the exhibition "Yield: Making Fashion without Making Waste" (2011), Roberts developed a Subtraction Cut response to zero waste fashion design. The red and white Zero Waste Sub-Cut Dress is made from 7 meters (7.6 yards) of two contrasting-colored fabrics and can be worn in at least five different ways, thereby further reducing waste by providing the wearer with multiple styles from a single purchase. While not entirely without fabric waste, the dress explores his innovative pattern cutting process in order to drastically reduce the waste generated without compromising the ethos of his approach. He uses the lining pattern pieces as the subtracted forms

from the outer garment, meaning these pieces function as both form making and garment finishing. The garment drapes and wraps the body in swathes of cloth and only reveals its form when on the body, creating tunnels for the body to travel through while affecting the exterior view of the garment. The contrasting fabrics reveal the twists and turns of the cloth as the cutting process distorts and rotates the dress front from back, inside to outside, plan to elevation. The connection between body and garment, owner and purchase, is important to Roberts and to own a sub-cut dress you need to make it yourself or work with the designer in collaboration.

46A

FIGURE 46A.
Zero waste subtraction cut dress by Julian Roberts (2010) can be worn more than seven different ways. Upon being invited to create a zero waste dress for the Yield exhibition, Roberts wanted to create a dress that someone could make their own. In this case, subtraction cutting and zero waste fashion design (or in essence, creative pattern cutting) provided an opportunity to design for user customization. Julian Roberts.

FIGURE 46B.
Julian Roberts (2010) user
modifiable zero waste subtraction
cut dress, shown in one of its
seven iterations. Julian Roberts;
Photograph by Thomas McQuillan.

46B

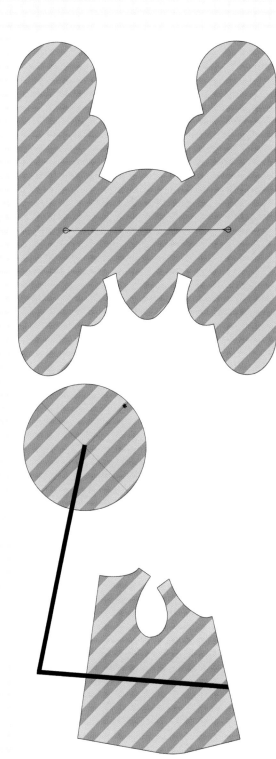

Lining Patterns

Shell patterns

FIGURE 47.
Pattern for Roberts' subtraction cut dress for Yield (2010). The arrow shows the direction of the body traveling through the garment. Julian Roberts.

47

THE CUTTING CIRCLE, 2011

In 2011 we (McQuillan, Rissanen, and Roberts) collaborated on a two-week research project, titled "The Cutting Circle." Our aim was to see how our mix of expertise in cutting techniques could reveal new ways of working and understanding our practices. Importantly, it revealed a marked difference in the way we authors worked, despite operating with the shared goal of eliminating fabric waste. This demonstrated that there was more than one way of doing zero waste. Reflecting on the experience was an important aspect of the project, and the project is ongoing (McQuillan, Rissanen, and Roberts 2013).

FIGURE 48.
Julian Roberts cutting out a Body Ruler, derived from the body of the intended wearer. Julian Roberts; Photograph by Timo Rissanen.

48

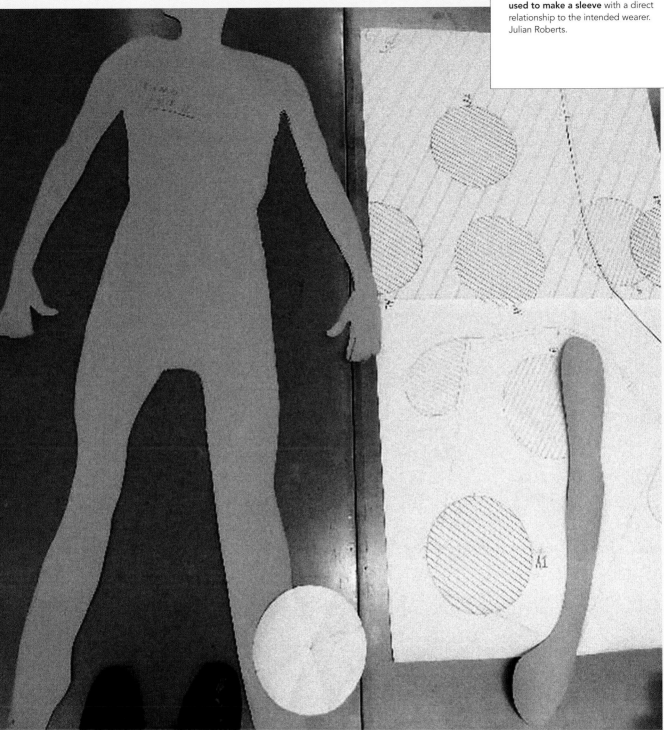

FIGURE 49.
Julian Roberts's Body Ruler was then
used to make a sleeve with a direct
relationship to the intended wearer.
Julian Roberts.

49

Cut one

Back

Front

Front

Front

Front

Cut one pair

Collar

Collar

Cut one pair

Collar

FIGURE 50.
Shirt collaboration by Holly McQuillan and Julian Roberts (2011) using the sleeve pattern cut with the Body Ruler. Pattern and photograph by Holly McQuillan.

50

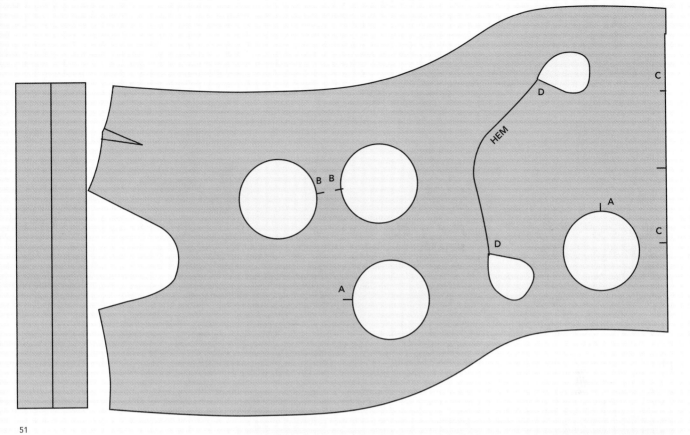

51

FIGURE 51.
The sleeve pattern used to make the "lost luggage trousers" for Timo Rissanen, by Julian Roberts (2010). Julian Roberts.

FIGURE 52.
The first toile of a failed pair of subtraction cutting trousers by Timo Rissanen, on the second day of "The Cutting Circle" (2011). Julian Roberts; Photograph by Timo Rissanen.

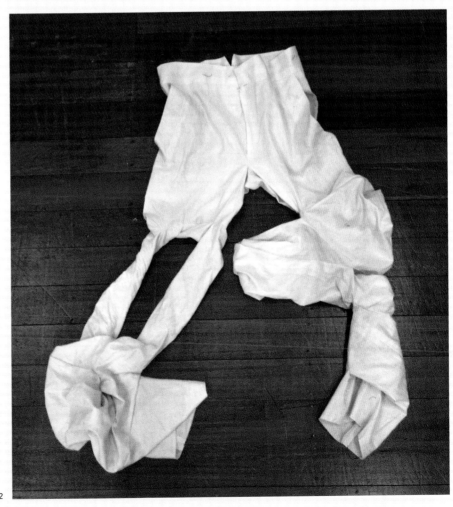

52

FIGURE 53.
Paper folding as design ideation, by David Valencia (2014). In the zero waste course taught by Timo Rissanen, students experiment with paper folding to generate ideas, alongside the more traditional methods of sketching and draping. The students' own initials form the cut lines in the paper. David Valencia.

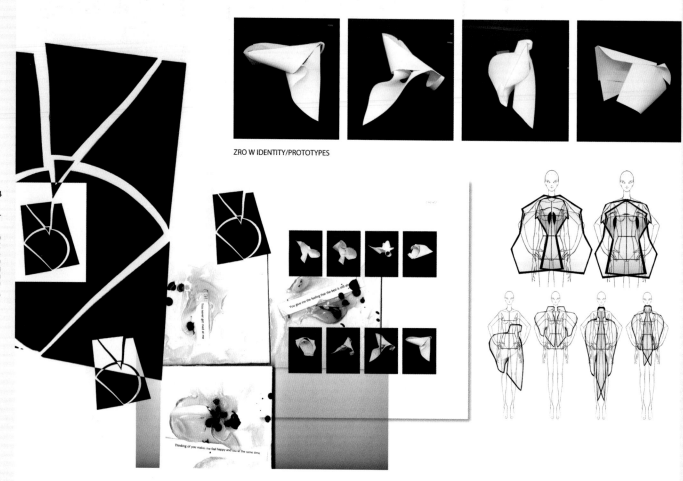

ZRO W IDENTITY/PROTOTYPES

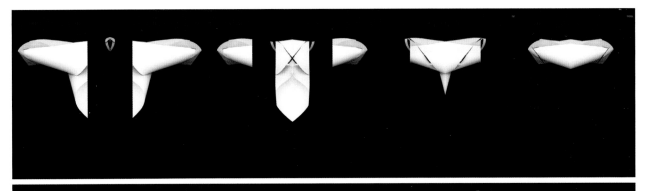

FIGURE 54.
David Valencia (2014) uses Photoshop to manipulate photographs of the paper folds into forms that begin to suggest garment shapes. David Valencia.

PATTERNS IN DESIGN IDEATION

In zero waste fashion design, pattern cutting is a design ideation tool, alongside the conventional sketching and draping. Here are examples of approaches that may be found useful in this respect. You are welcome to copy these approaches. The ultimate aim is to inspire you to experiment and come up with your own approaches.

Within the class on zero waste fashion design at Parsons, Rissanen asks the students to write their initials on a piece of paper—A4 and US letter size work well. The students cut through the lines of the initials and tape the pieces into three-dimensional shapes. These may resemble parts of garments; often they do not.

The students photograph these shapes from multiple angles, and print out the photographs. These provide a rich starting point for further designing, whether through pattern cutting, draping or sketching. This process is mirrored with an approach McQuillan has used that produces garment forms from the shapes generated or inspired by words and typeface.

In War/Peace the two dresses are designed from a starting point of the words war and peace spelled in Helvetica; through manipulation of the typeface and placement of the text, fabric manipulation, and a digital textile print of the words, the garments are developed.

FIGURE 55.
Designed in response to brief exploring notions of War/Peace in contemporary society, these dresses by Holly McQuillan (2012) utilize Helvetica type as a mark of the ubiquitousness of conflict. Holly McQuillan; Photograph by Thomas McQuillan.

55

FIGURE 56.
The patterns for the War/Peace dresses reveal typographic origins. The War dress pattern was developed by placing the neckline in the "R" and draping the remainder on the stand. Holly McQuillan.

56

57

Modular and tessellated approaches have been explored by a number of designers. McQuillan's process of tessellation is designed with the objective of using one pattern composed of a tessellating repeat, cut once through multiple layers of different cloths to produce an almost infinite number of possible garment designs through modular components. These can be returned to the designer and remade into new garments when the owner becomes dissatisfied or when fashion changes. This system enables the production of both tailored and fluid designs, depending on the configuration of the pieces and on the fabric used. By generating a repeating two-dimensional pattern that diminishes at the selvage, the marker generates minimal or no waste.

This design process is both risky and certain, as you cannot predict how the garment will look before the cloth is cut, but the designer has control over how to use each piece to form the final design. The process of applying these shapes to a dress form is more akin to sculpture than drape. Importantly it is an approach that requires a complete shift in the industry toward localized, smaller, and slower design approaches. It also encourages an intimacy between designer, producer, and consumer, uniting the three.

This is a shift from the dominant industry models of fashion design, using available technology and materials. Furthermore, the design can be disseminated freely, leading to global design distribution through local production, combined with designed-in aesthetic change coupled with reduced material use.

Selvedge

Selvedge

58

FIGURE 58.
Hyperbolic tessellation pattern is laser cut
from cloth and sculpted on a dress form. The
diminishing scale of the tesselated pattern allows
for a variety of piece sizes and the edges (in blue) to
be used as lace-like edging. Holly McQuillan.

☐ Garment body pieces

■ Decorative edging

Width: adjustable depending on fabric width
Length: as required by design

FIGURE 59.
The laser cut pieces are applied to the dress form in a process more akin to sculpture than pattern cutting. Holly McQuillan.

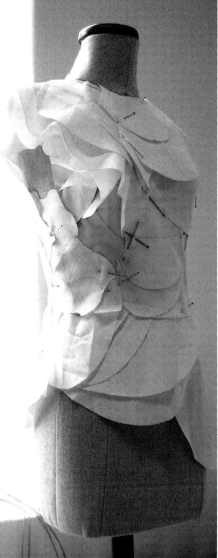

60

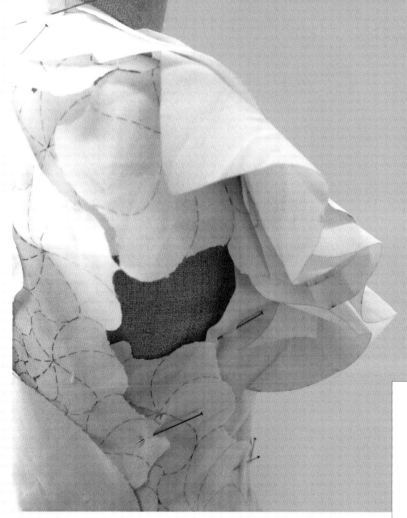

FIGURE 60.
When the design is no longer desired the pieces can be "re-sculpted" into a new design and damaged sections can be replaced individually. Holly McQuillan.

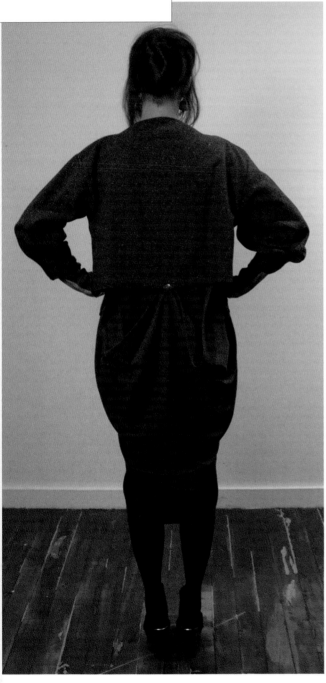

FIGURE 61.
Jacket by Study NY by Tara St James (2012). St James repeats successful shapes over time, refining them and adopting them to different fabrics, reminding us that good ideas do not have a use-by-date, even in fashion. Tara St James.

Two designers have experimented with rigid geometric shapes some twenty-five years apart. In the mid-1980s, Yoshiki Hishinuma (1986) created garments entirely from triangles of fabric. While the garments are not necessarily zero waste, Hishinuma's design approach has considerable potential in a zero waste context. In 2009 Tara St James showed the first collection of Study NY, titled "The Square Project," and each look was a geometric exercise. The first look on the runway was made from one square of fabric, the second from two squares, and so forth. The entire collection was zero waste.

Some garments from this collection are still being produced more than five years later, speaking to the relatively slow pace at which the brand operates in contrast to dominant fashion industry practices. Both designers' work show that placing somewhat arbitrary limitations on the design process can in fact result in highly original and plausible garments.

Squares and rectangles are the easiest shapes to work with in zero waste fashion design, because that is how fabric is shaped: woven cloth is a grid of warp and weft yarns. It is perfectly possible, however, to design with circles and curves. McQuillan's shirt and trousers based on a circle/oval from Void demonstrates how shapes generated by the curved trouser pattern, based on a pattern in *Pattern Magic* (Nakamichi 2010), creates a curved silhouette for the top.

A common misconception about zero waste fashion design is that it is limited to working with straight lines. Void and many other garments by Holly demonstrate that this need not be the case. Given how human bodies are shaped, and how cloth shaped by patterns responds to it, working with curves is inseparable from designing garments.

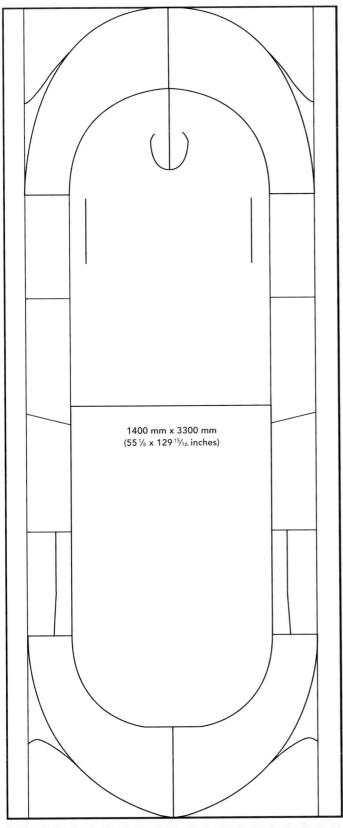

1400 mm x 3300 mm
(55 ⅛ x 129 ¹⁵⁄₁₆ inches)

62

63

FIGURES 62 AND 63.
Void: Arc T-shirt and trousers designed by Holly McQuillan following a collaborative research project with Julian Roberts and Timo Rissanen (2011). The starting point of this design was inspired by the Orange Peel trousers from the *Pattern Magic* series of books. Figure 62: Holly McQuillan; Figure 63: Holly McQuillan; Photograph by Thomas McQuillan.

This chapter has demonstrated that pattern cutting can be a creative activity. In zero waste fashion design it needs to be a creative and generative process. While this may initially seem challenging for designers and fashion educators who have primarily viewed pattern cutting as a technical process that supports design, the shift in perception is in fact an easy one to make.

1150 mm x 2570 mm
(45 ¼ x 101 ³⁄₁₆ inches)

FIGURE 64.
Void: Collaboration shirt (2011) designed by Holly McQuillan following "The Cutting Circle" (a collaborative research project with Timo Rissanen and Julian Roberts). The sleeves explore Roberts subtraction cutting methods as applied to zero waste. Holly McQuillan.

SHORT CUTS

1 Speculate on the advantages and disadvantages of the conventional fashion role hierarchy.

2 Propose a range of alternative arrangements of the roles within fashion industry to better enable zero waste fashion within industry.

3 Speculate on the relationship between conventional and creative pattern cutting and their place within zero waste fashion design. What are the tensions, and what are the opportunities?

zero waste fashion design: the basics

This chapter focuses on successful strategies and techniques for zero waste fashion design. Through practice over time, you will likely come up with your own techniques that work for you. Embrace risk in design as an access to new solutions; taking risks creates new possibilities. Designing within, and with, the fabric is integral to this kind of designing. In zero waste fashion design, fabric creates the space for inventive exploration.

FIGURE 65A.
Hoodie and jeans by Timo Rissanen
(2008). The cut of the hoodie is
based on Vionnet's cutting, while
the jeans are based on Thayaht's
tuta. Timo Rissanen; Photograph by
Mariano Garcia.

FIGURE 65B.
Hoodie by Timo Rissanen (2008).
Exploring the body pieces on the fabric width revealed the triangle shapes that became the hood in this garment. Timo Rissanen.

FIGURE 65C.
Completed hoodie pattern by Timo Rissanen (2008). In the final design stages space was created between the two body pieces to create the facing and waist casing pieces. Timo Rissanen.

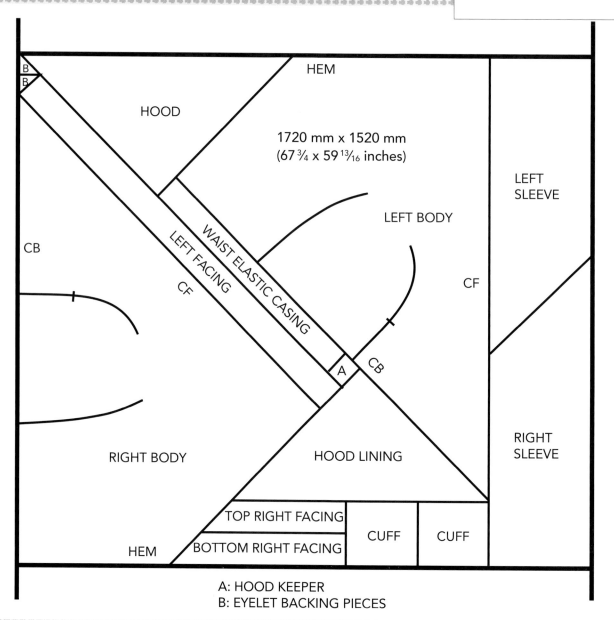

HEM

HOOD

B
B

1720 mm x 1520 mm
(67 ¾ x 59 ¹³⁄₁₆ inches)

LEFT SLEEVE

LEFT BODY

CB

WAIST ELASTIC CASING

LEFT FACING

CF

CF

A

CB

RIGHT SLEEVE

RIGHT BODY

HOOD LINING

TOP RIGHT FACING

HEM

BOTTOM RIGHT FACING

CUFF

CUFF

A: HOOD KEEPER
B: EYELET BACKING PIECES

65C

CRITERIA FOR ZERO WASTE FASHION DESIGN

There are five primary criteria to negotiate during the zero waste fashion design process: aesthetics, fit, cost, fabric waste, and manufacturability. These depend on context. Just as different sets of criteria may be appropriate in different contexts, the criteria may bear different weights depending on context and the stage of design process you are in. However, the elimination of fabric waste should never be used to justify a compromise in aesthetics or fit; nor should it result in undue increase in manufacturing cost, for example, due to unnecessarily complicated construction.

While the focus in this book is on fabric waste, it is best thought of as one of countless facets of sustainability. Sustainability in fashion is complex, just as the fashion industry is complex. It is imperative within any company that this complexity is acknowledged and embraced; any complex problem likely requires multiple solutions of different scales. Explorations in zero waste fashion design need to move beyond singular solutions and integrate with other solutions to enrich and engage the experience of fashion for everyone, from the industry to users of fashion.

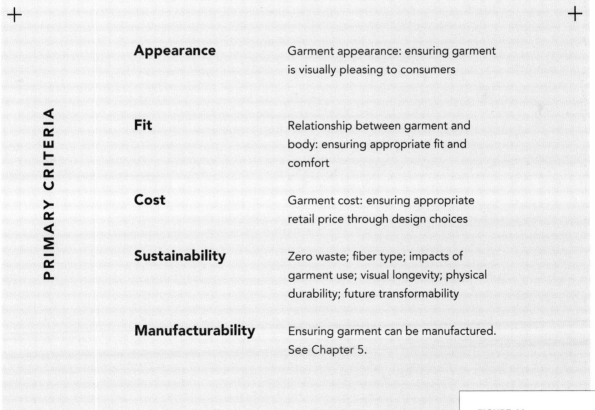

PRIMARY CRITERIA		
Appearance	Garment appearance: ensuring garment is visually pleasing to consumers
Fit	Relationship between garment and body: ensuring appropriate fit and comfort
Cost	Garment cost: ensuring appropriate retail price through design choices
Sustainability	Zero waste; fiber type; impacts of garment use; visual longevity; physical durability; future transformability
Manufacturability	Ensuring garment can be manufactured. See Chapter 5.

FIGURE 66.
Criteria for zero waste fashion design. Timo Rissanen; Holly McQuillan.

Often when sustainability is discussed in relation to fashion, the first point of access for people is the material: the provenance of the fiber and the type of dye, for example. Materials are a tangible and significant component of fashion, and the sustainability of a material is relatively easy to study and grasp. However, fashion is a method of interrelated, overlapping systems of material flows, manufacturing, commerce, garment-use practices, and disposal, to name a few. It is necessary to focus on details and single parts of the messy overall system, as is done in this book. In doing so, however, it is important to always examine the part in the overall context.

Fletcher (2014: 71–85) provides a useful, fashion-focused overview of Donella Meadows's list of places to intervene in a system in order to transform that system. According to Meadows, the mindset or paradigm is the most effective place to intervene. The mindset that requires particular attention in regards to sustainability, including fabric waste, in fashion is a redesign of fashion design and its role in the fashion industry and in society in general. Zero waste fashion design is one useful tool in shifting the fashion paradigm.

THE DESIGN IDEATION TOOLBOX

Every fashion designer works differently; there is no correct way to generate garment ideas or to refine and develop those ideas into resolved pieces. The same applies to zero waste fashion design. As Aakko and Niinimäki (2014: 75) note: "Taking distance from the common rules of pattern making allows experimental and creative design processes." What distinguishes zero waste fashion design from conventional fashion design is that pattern cutting must be integral to the design process; pattern cutting is fashion design.

The end goal, the kind of garment to be designed and made, suggests some starting points. For example, if the designer feels that a particular feature or specific fit must be in the garment (a specific sleeve or a collar, for example), then that would be a consideration from the start. First, the pattern would be made for this feature. While doing this, the designer should be mindful of the negative spaces that any pattern pieces form, as eventually they, too, will become a part of a pattern piece or pieces. Once the toile for that part has been fitted and the pattern corrected, you can begin to explore

the pattern piece or pieces on the fabric width to see how they might place in relation to the selvages and to each other. This will begin to reveal the negative spaces that open the door for further design exploration.

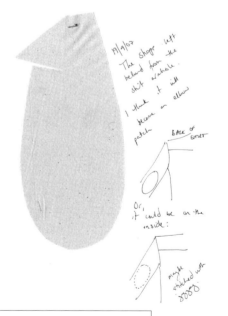

67

FIGURE 67.
Speculation on negative space created by an armhole by Timo Rissanen (2007). This eventually became a sleeve placket. Timo Rissanen.

ZWPC WORKSHOP, AALTO 2012

McQuillan's workshop at Aalto University in 2012 (Aakko and Niinimäki 2014: 71) presented the participants with three approaches that are helpful starting points for anyone wanting to experiment with zero waste fashion design. Planned Chaos uses conventional garment blocks as the starting point, Geo Cut begins with abstract shapes and geometry, while Cut and Drape is a free-form approach of working on a dress form. Each can be used independently, and in early exploration it may make sense to do that; however, over time, various combinations of the three are likely to provide the richest results. Most of the authors' works in this book are examples of these approaches, or combinations of them.

68

FIGURE 68.
Dress by Varvara Zhemchuzhnikova designed and hand printed during the ZWPC workshop at Aalto University in 2012. Kirsi Niinimäki.

ZERO WASTE BLOCKS

Most books on pattern cutting show how to draft basic blocks or slopers. The use of the terms varies on the region and the context, whether an educational institution, company, or a textbook. Sloper is the dominant term in North American fashion education, while block is used elsewhere. Fasanella (2006) distinguishes these clearly: a sloper does not include seam allowance, while a block does. As an example of regional differences, in New Zealand the word block is used, but this does not include seam allowance. Blocks are discussed here, because the seam allowance is visually, as well as physically, included in each pattern piece, making the process easier. Exploring how these pieces might interlock on fabric can be challenging if you have to imagine seam allowances in place, as opposed to already having them there.

Although the term "basic block" is often used, a block pattern is a subjective construct. Within a company a block pattern will reflect the desired fit of the company's core customer. Elements of fit, for example, the amount of ease or the height of the underarm of an armhole, are dependent on the context of the company. As for design, as Fasanella (2006) notes, a block is a pattern of a style that sells well. A block pattern therefore hints at the company's overall aesthetic. The blocks that the authors have developed for their respective practices speak of the kind of garments they design.

Most books on pattern drafting present blocks (or slopers) as if they are a neutral ground from which to build a garment. However, Lindqvist (2013) has pointed out that such blocks are not neutral. Rather, blocks assume a series of rules about dressing the body in a Western industrial context: the blocks have side and shoulder seams, "fixed" dart positions, and a particular amount of ease. Blocks are useful tools: an appropriate block is selected according to garment type, material, and the desired fit, and it is manipulated to reflect the desired design. Blocks assist with the timely development of new garment styles, and they assure consistent fit in garments over time. Within the context of zero waste fashion design, conventional blocks can be used in a similar way; however, we propose another way of considering zero waste garment blocks.

A zero waste garment block accounts for the eventual pattern layout, the marker, of a garment in some way. For example, corresponding edges of two pattern pieces may align perfectly while ensuring that each piece remains on the desired grain. Reducing complexity in designing the final marker is partially built into the block. During the design process, a zero waste garment block is modified for the desired design details, fit, and fabric width of the final garment.

A useful strategy throughout the design process is to keep a list of the eventual pattern pieces for the desired design. As each piece is developed, it helps to mark on each pattern piece which areas are fixed and which are "flexible." For example, for a particular fit and silhouette certain seams are likely to be fixed, while the shape of the loose edge of a facing may have some flexibility. This flexibility helps in resolving the overall pattern layout of a zero waste garment. Through the design process these fixed and flexible areas work in tandem with each other, each influencing the other, while accounting for the fabric width and the goals the designer has for the garment.

One aspect of zero waste fashion design that requires attention is regarding facings and seam and edge finishes. These need to be part of the design process throughout. Leaving them to a late stage in the process will not work, as they have specific implications for the pattern pieces (for example, in terms of allowance width), which in turn impact on the overall layout of the pieces.

In her research McQuillan has developed a series of setups, which she uses to base many of her designs on. Two are discussed in detail, and illustrations of others are for you to explore.

TABLE OF KEY CONSIDERATIONS

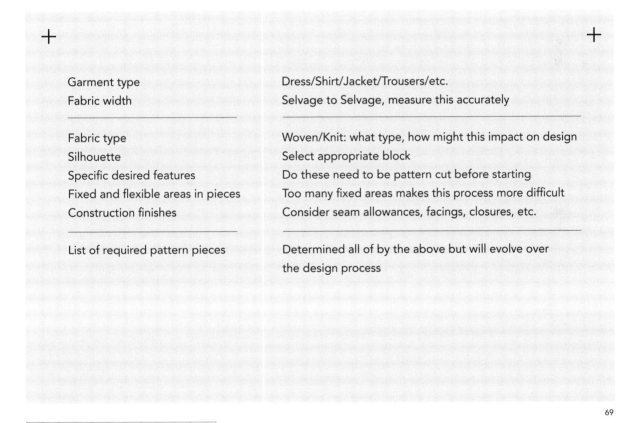

Garment type	Dress/Shirt/Jacket/Trousers/etc.
Fabric width	Selvage to Selvage, measure this accurately
Fabric type	Woven/Knit: what type, how might this impact on design
Silhouette	Select appropriate block
Specific desired features	Do these need to be pattern cut before starting
Fixed and flexible areas in pieces	Too many fixed areas makes this process more difficult
Construction finishes	Consider seam allowances, facings, closures, etc.
List of required pattern pieces	Determined all of by the above but will evolve over the design process

69

FIGURE 69.
Table of key considerations: specific desired features; list of eventual pattern pieces; fixed and flexible areas in pieces; construction finishes. Timo Rissanen; Holly McQuillan.

T-SHIRT/TUNIC
SETUP

FIGURE 70.
T-shirt/tunic setup,
developed from examples
found throughout history.
Photograph by Thomas
McQuillan.

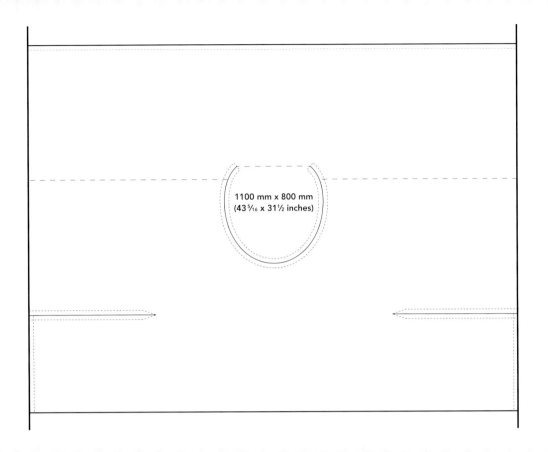

1100 mm x 800 mm
(43 5/16 x 31 1/2 inches)

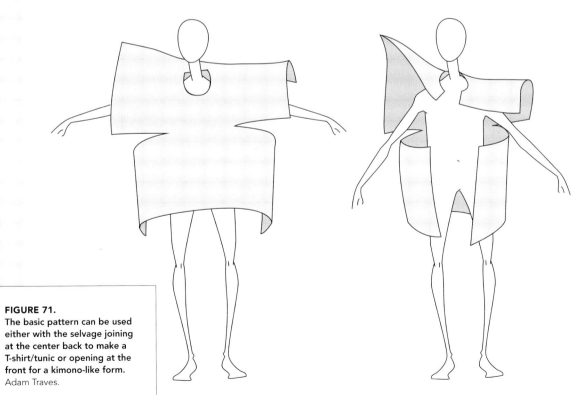

FIGURE 71.
The basic pattern can be used either with the selvage joining at the center back to make a T-shirt/tunic or opening at the front for a kimono-like form.
Adam Traves.

TRAPEZE SLEEVELESS TUNIC
by Holly McQuillan

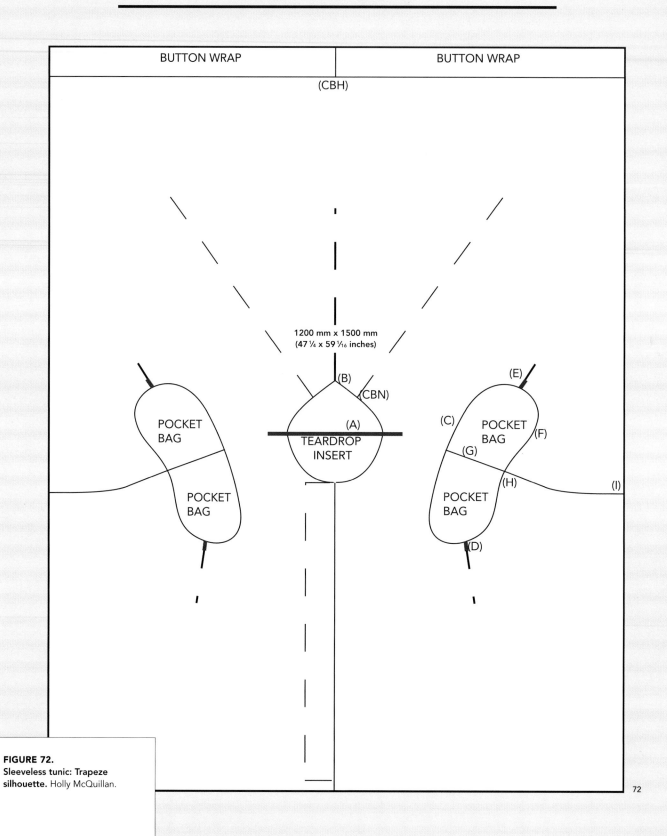

BUTTON WRAP

BUTTON WRAP

(CBH)

1200 mm x 1500 mm
(47 ¼ x 59 ¹⁄₁₆ inches)

(B)

(CBN)

(E)

(C)

POCKET
BAG

POCKET
BAG

(A)

TEARDROP
INSERT

(F)

(G)

POCKET
BAG

(H)

POCKET
BAG

(I)

(D)

CHAPTER 3

FIGURE 72.
Sleeveless tunic: Trapeze
silhouette. Holly McQuillan.

This design is developed through the Planned Chaos approach and revolves around the simple placement of neckline and armholes. It can be modified in many ways to generate a range of outcomes and silhouettes. It combines flat pattern cutting with drape to develop the design to its final realization. The block used is usually a darted bodice block, but it can also be a shirt or blouse block, even a jacket block. The block will be determined by the final goals of the project. If you aim to resolve the design into a shirt, then begin with a block with sleeves. The key fixed areas will be the relationship between neckline and armholes and the armhole/sleeve crown relationship. Fabric length is twice the length of the garment, and the width the volume of cloth available to the designer to achieve the trapeze silhouette. For example, using a 200-centimeter-long (78¾ inches) length of cloth will result in a top that is 100 centimeters (39⅜ inches) from shoulder to hem. A narrow cloth results in a less voluminous trapeze design. There is also a potential direct relationship between the width of the fabric, which determines the button placket (button wrap) length, and the length of the center-front opening where the button placket is sewn.

This is a setup for a sleeveless tunic design with a center-front opening with button placket and inseam pockets. It uses a piece of cloth 120 centimeters wide and 150 centimeters long (47¼ × 59 inches). As it is symmetrical, it is folded along the grain line, to measure 60 centimeters by 150 centimeters (23⅝ × 59 inches).

Detailed instructions:

1 Begin with a darted bodice block and pivot the darts out of the shoulders and into the waist. This is the starting point of the trapeze silhouette and allows for the shoulder seams to

be eliminated. There can be a direct relationship between the half width of the fabric (which determines the button wrap length) and the length of the center-front opening, where the button wrap is sewn.

2 Mark out a rectangle half the width (60 centimeters/23⅝ inches) by the full length of the cloth (150 centimeters/59 inches). Label selvage (sl), fold line (fl), and top and bottom cut edges (tc and bc). Six centimeters (2⅜ inches) down from (tc), draw a straight line parallel to this. Label as button wrap (2 centimeters [¾ inch] button wrap with 1 centimeter [⅜ inch] seam allowance). Mark center-back hem (cbh). Mark (a) approximately halfway from button wrap to bottom cut edge (72 centimeters/28⅜ inches). Place the center front of front bodice block one centimeter from (fl), aligning shoulder/neck point with (a). Place darted bodice on the back, aligning shoulder seams so as to eliminate them; mark in position of center-back neck (cbn) point.

3 Widen neckline 5 millimeters (³⁄₁₆ inch) all the way around, and extend the back neckline to the (fl) (b). This teardrop shape becomes an insert, which supports the back drape form.

4 Mark around front and back armhole (c), marking the side seams ([d] and [e]). Continue the back armhole around in a smooth rounded line to join the front armhole (f); this forms the pocket bags when divided in two (g), so ensure a hand will fit comfortably inside.

5 Measure from shoulder around (f), and mark at halfway point (h). Extend a line at a right angle, and then curve toward selvage (i).

6 Cut garment, sew cut line (f), attaching (e)–(h) to (d)–(h). Sew back pleat (b) + (cbn). Insert teardrop insert at (cbh), then resolve final design on mannequin, considering button wrap and pocket placement.

The length of front and back is determined by the placement of the armhole and neckline; moving these toward the front hem will generate a shorter front and longer back. The same mechanism can be used to orient the fullness toward a particular axis of the design.

FIGURE 73.
Alternative layout of Trapeze tunic setup; by moving the neckline and armholes, fullness can be redistributed to any axis of the body. Holly McQuillan.

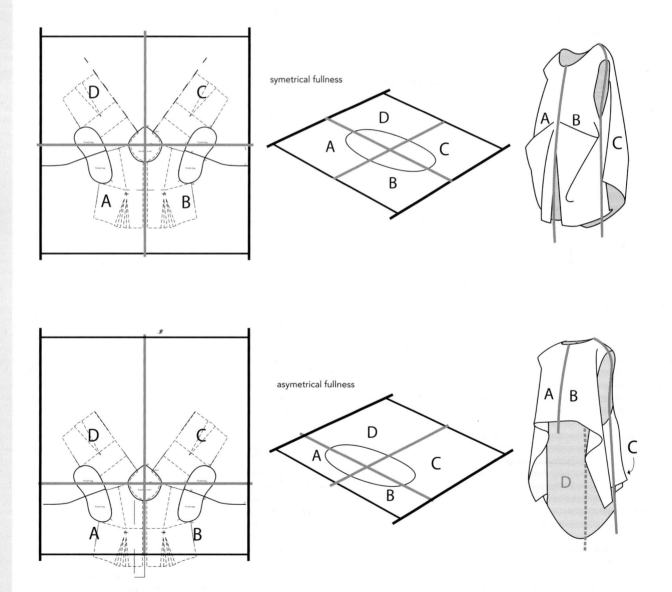

symetrical fullness

asymetrical fullness

74A

FIGURE 74A.
Trapeze tunic setup: fullness
distributed to backs (2014).
Holly McQuillan; Photograph by
Thomas McQuillan.

74B

FIGURE 74B.
Trapeze tunic setup: centrally
oriented fullness (2014).
Holly McQuillan; Photograph by
Thomas McQuillan.

SQUARES AS SLEEVES

FIGURE 75
The large square cut sleeve drops almost to the waist and generates a kimono form.
Holly McQuillan; Photograph by Thomas McQuillan.

Wrap tie

Wrap tie

Sleeve

Sleeve

Neck

Body

Back skirt/wrap

Back skirt/wrap

99

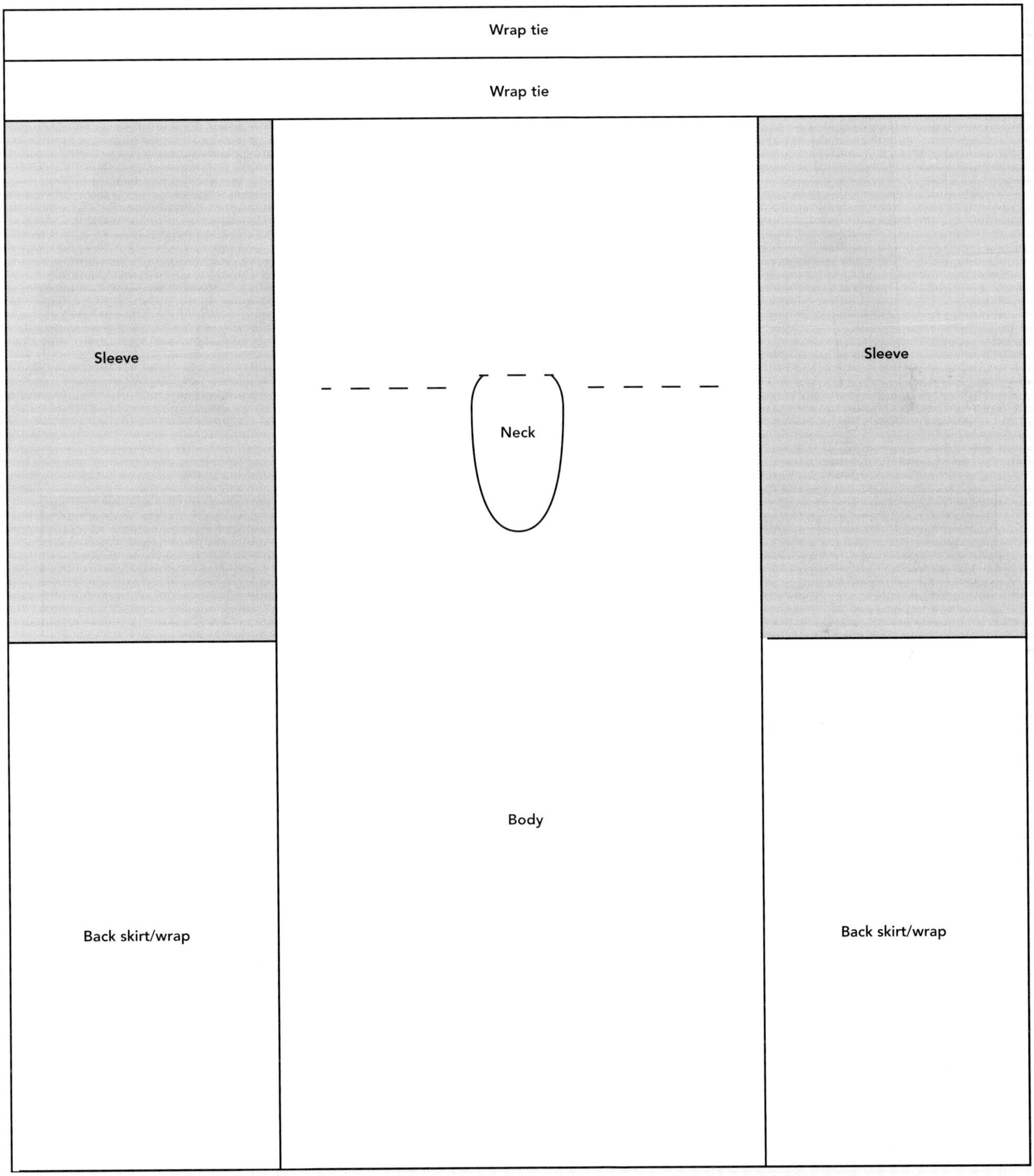

TRIANGLES AS SLEEVES

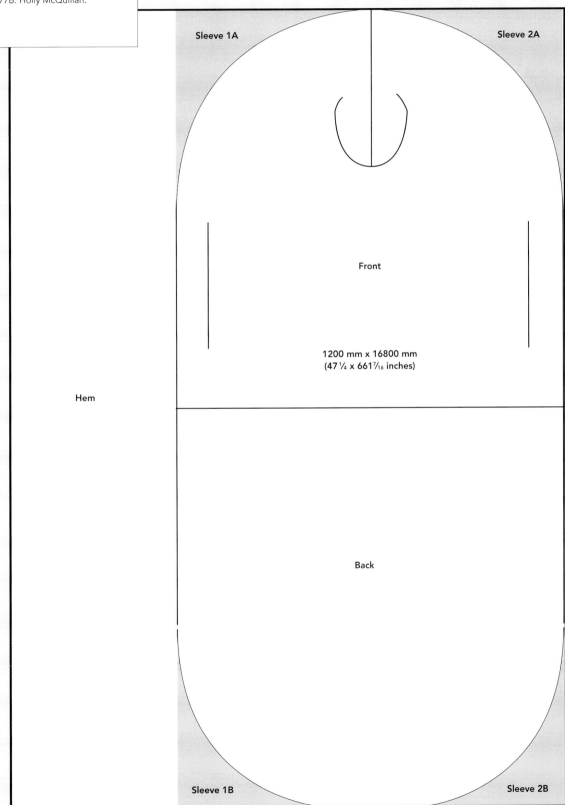

FIGURES 77A AND 77B.
Triangles as sleeves: arc T-shirt pattern detail, Void (2012). By twisting the triangle pattern piece into a tapered tube form, a sleeve is able to be constructed. Figure 77A: Photograph by Thomas McQuillan. Figure 77B: Holly McQuillan.

Sleeve 1A

Sleeve 2A

Front

1200 mm x 16800 mm
(47 ¼ x 661⁷⁄₁₆ inches)

Hem

Back

Sleeve 1B

Sleeve 2B

77B

SLEEVE BLOCKS AS SLEEVES

78A

FIGURES 78A AND 78B.
Sleeve blocks as sleeves: men's
hoodie pattern sleeve shown in gray.
Dividing the sleeve block into sections
can allow for more design options
when developing zero waste patterns.
Figure 78A: Photograph by Thomas
McQuillan. Figure 78B: Holly McQuillan.

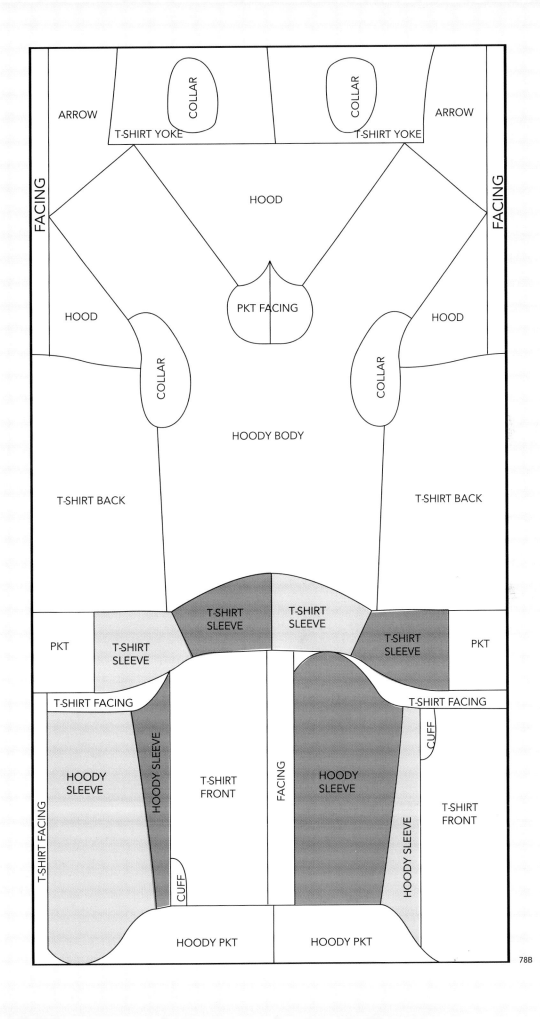

78B

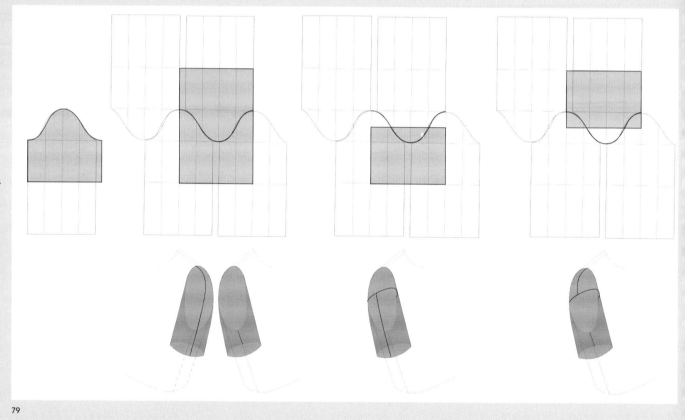

79

FIGURE 79.
Translating a set-in sleeve form into rectangles to enable easier arrangement within a zero waste pattern. Holly McQuillan.

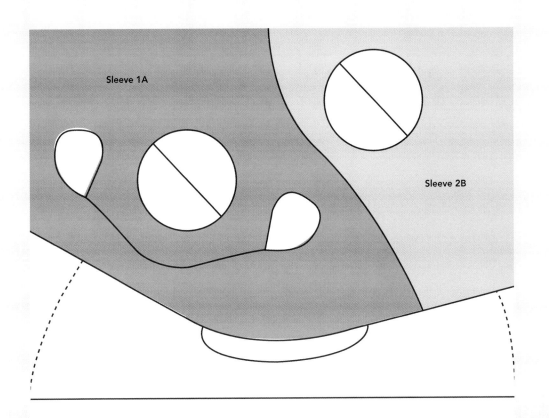

Sleeve 1A

Sleeve 2B

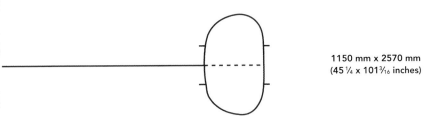

1150 mm x 2570 mm
(45 ¼ x 101 ³⁄₁₆ inches)

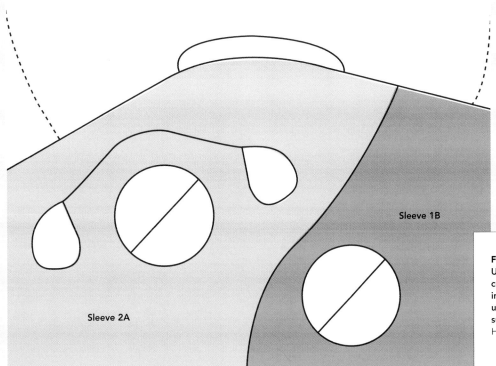

Sleeve 1B

Sleeve 2A

FIGURE 80.
Using only the sleeve crown to ensure it will fit into armhole, developed using Julian Roberts's subtraction cutting approach. Holly McQuillan.

ENDURANCE SHIRT
by Timo Rissanen

81

2 The yokes are divided at center back for flexibility within the marker; placed together they form a rectangular module within the marker. Having two pairs of yokes rather than one pair allows also for later alteration of the shirt through the center back.

3 Analyze what is fixed: in this case, the relationship between the two body pieces, the two sleeve caps, and the four yokes pieces are independently fixed. You can now examine how these, along with the lower sleeves, might place and interact on the width of the fabric. Have also the list of eventual pieces handy. Usually a shirt has sleeve plackets, cuffs, a collar with stand, perhaps a pocket, and so forth. Keep in mind what is fixed and what is flexible. For example, the edge of a cuff that joins to the sleeve is a fixed measurement. However, the outer edge of the cuff can be any shape you desire it to be. Having these fixed and flexible components listed, together with the list of pieces, makes the design process more efficient.

1 Develop the body and sleeve patterns. One sleeve has the seam at underarm, the other at outer arm. This allows the interlocking of the two sleeve caps. The front yoke seams are on the cross grain, at a 90-degree angle from center front. This allows the two body pieces to be placed next to each other. The most challenging part is to achieve a satisfactory fit for the armhole and sleeve while achieving the interlocking of the two sleeve caps. If a choice has to be made between wastage and fit, fit should govern the final sleeve piece. This shirt has rectangular sleeves, which are tapered with tucks; darts could also be used. A firm shirting fabric would likely require a tapered shape if excess volume is to be avoided.

4 Keep designing the remaining components of the shirt. For his shirt Rissanen used the round shapes created by the yokes for half of the cuff. The other half came from a rectangle within the marker. This shirt also required an internal stay for the back pleat, as well as an internal belt to create a blouson effect at the back. One of the sleeve plackets came from the oval created by the armhole, while the other placket is a more conventional rectangle.

FIGURE 81.
Endurance shirt by Timo Rissanen (2009). The shirt is designed with future repair and alteration in mind. Timo Rissanen; Photograph by Silversalt.

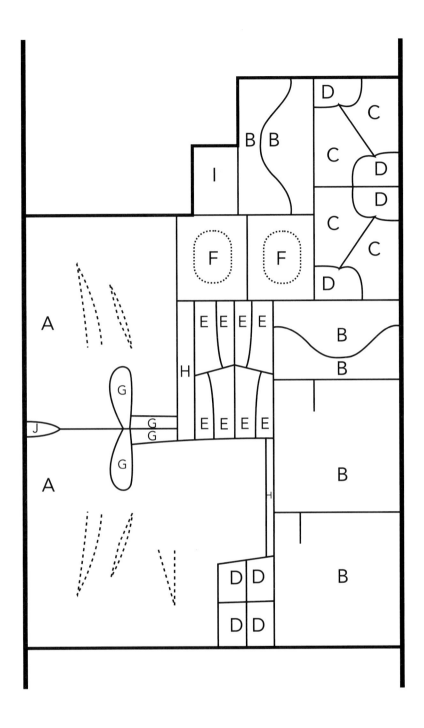

Endurance Shirt I
Fabric: 100% Linen
Fabric width: 135 cm
Yield: 176 cm

A: Body
B: Sleeve (including top sleeve lining)
C: Yoke
D: Cuff
E: Collar & stand
F: Elbow patch
G: Sleeve placket
H: Internal waist stay
I: Internal back pleat stay
J: CB Yoke appliqué

FIGURE 82.
Pattern of the Endurance shirt.
"Excess" fabric is built into the elbow patches to facilitate future repair, while seams in the yoke and collar would allow enlarging the shirt if needed. Timo Rissanen.

TAILORED JACKET
by Holly McQuillan

This setup, with two-piece sleeve dissecting the body, can be used for menswear and womenswear to achieve a tailored jacket with two-piece sleeve, with fabrics that have flexibility with the grain line. Fit is controlled by the block you start with and the way you deal with negative space to form the lapel, collar, pockets, and so on. McQuillan has used this as a basis for a motorbike jacket, frock coat, men's soft structured jacket, and men's and women's tailored jacket and trouser sets (where both garment patterns are embedded in a single pattern). This layout uses a three-piece jacket block with two-piece sleeve.

Detailed instructions:

1 Measure out the width of cloth. This needs to be at least twice the top sleeve length, including seam allowances. If longer, the hem can be deeper to accommodate the extra cloth width, or you can use the space between the top sleeve hem and the selvage to generate a welt pocket or other details.

2 Place the jacket back at the center line, and align side body to back so the pieces meet at armhole; pivot to eliminate the seam. Do the same with front body/side body as shown, pivoting out the front shoulder dart. You can leave the seam at the front/side body to insert a pocket, or add a seam elsewhere later for this purpose. Measure (a)–(b).

3 Place top sleeve so distance from (c)–(d) is the same as (a)–(b) (as pictured) and so the sleeve crowns touch and hems are parallel to selvage.

4 Section off the top section of the undersleeve as shown (adding seam allowances). Place remainder of undersleeve at back waist as shown.

83

FIGURE 83.
Many variations are possible from the same basic tailored jacket setup. Here a stand collar transitions into a draped and darted lapel. Holly McQuillan; Photograph by Thomas McQuillan.

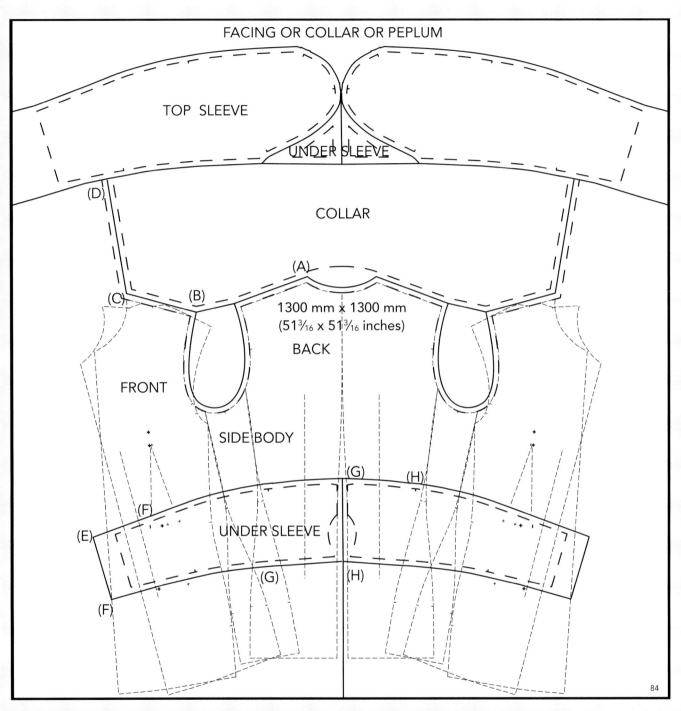

FACING OR COLLAR OR PEPLUM

TOP SLEEVE

UNDER SLEEVE

(D)

COLLAR

(A)

(C) (B)

1300 mm x 1300 mm
(51³⁄₁₆ x 51³⁄₁₆ inches)

BACK

FRONT

SIDE BODY

(G) (H)

(F)

(E)

UNDER SLEEVE

(G) (H)

(F)

84

Sewing Notes:

When sewing the waist seam, match (e) to (f) and overlap at back (g)–(h).

Notes:

The space above top sleeve is available for use as a facing for the hem, additional peplum detail, or collar, depending on the desired design. Length of the jacket is determined by the length of the cloth used, and silhouette can be manipulated by the placement of the undersleeve: place the sleeve lower down and you can achieve a dropped waist silhouette, higher up and an empire style is possible. On a men's jacket, you can extend the cut line from the top and bottom of the undersleeve to the selvage to produce a pocket bag, therefore eliminating the sculptural form created.

FIGURE 84.
Tailored jacket setup (two-piece sleeve dissecting body).
Holly McQuillan.

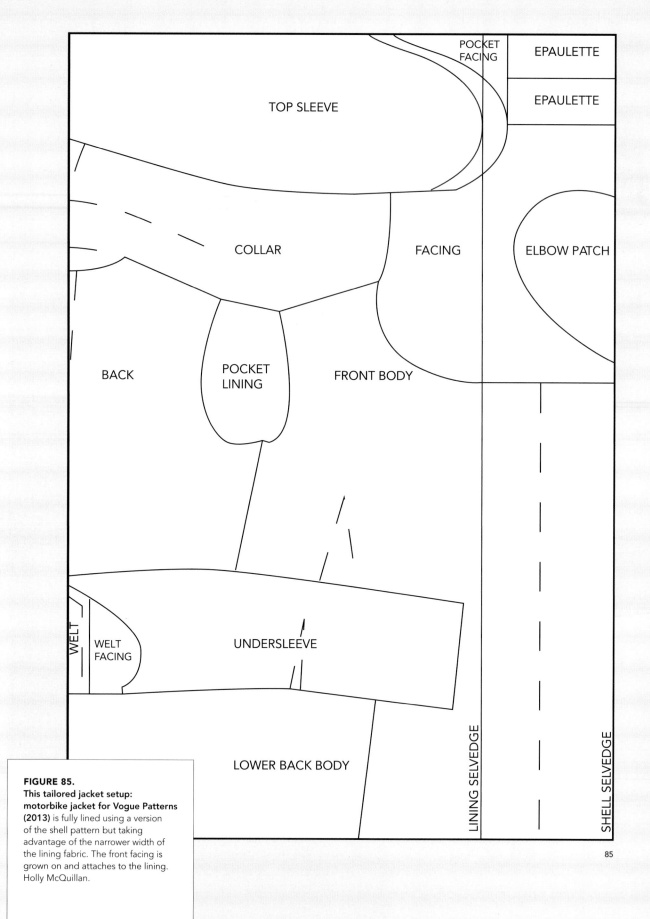

POCKET
FACING

EPAULETTE

EPAULETTE

TOP SLEEVE

COLLAR

FACING

ELBOW PATCH

BACK

POCKET
LINING

FRONT BODY

WELT

WELT
FACING

UNDERSLEEVE

LOWER BACK BODY

LINING SELVEDGE

SHELL SELVEDGE

FIGURE 85.
This tailored jacket setup:
motorbike jacket for Vogue Patterns
(2013) is fully lined using a version
of the shell pattern but taking
advantage of the narrower width of
the lining fabric. The front facing is
grown on and attaches to the lining.
Holly McQuillan.

85

FIGURE 86.
The motorbike jacket was developed from a favorite piece designed by New Zealand label WORLD and owned by Holly McQuillan. When redesigning the pattern, Holly aimed to maintain the essence of the original design while achieving a zero waste outcome. Holly McQuillan.

FIGURE 87.
This tailored men's jacket + trouser "set" from Void (2012) utilizes a very similar foundational setup to the women's tailored jacket setup. The pattern was developed as a two-piece suit, whereby the trouser and jacket are cut from a single zero waste pattern. Holly McQuillan; Photograph by Thomas McQuillan.

PATTERN SETUPS
by Holly McQuillan

The following setups are offered as visual starting points for you to experiment with. Remember: the only mistake you can make is not to try them out!

SIMPLE TROUSER
SETUP

88A

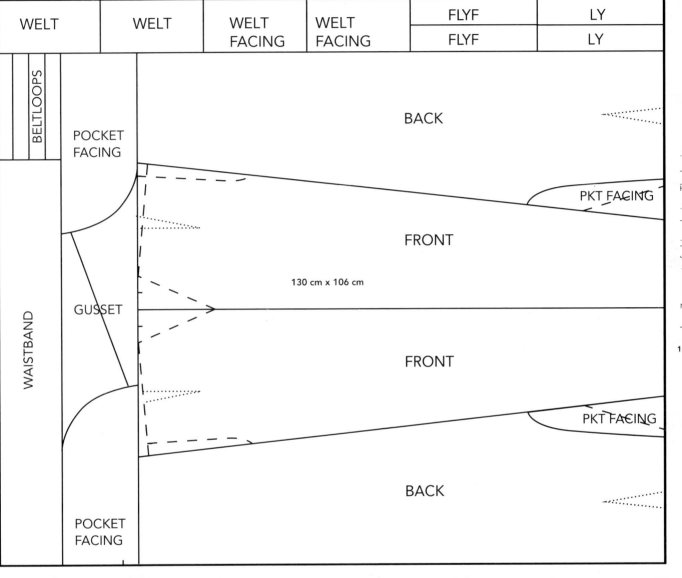

WELT		WELT		WELT FACING	WELT FACING	FLYF	LY
						FLYF	LY

BELTLOOPS

POCKET FACING

BACK

PKT FACING

FRONT

130 cm x 106 cm

WAISTBAND

GUSSET

FRONT

PKT FACING

BACK

POCKET FACING

88B

FIGURES 88A AND 88B.
Simple trouser setup: tapered leg trouser (2014). In this pattern the front and back legs are nested with each other and the upper thigh/crotch fit is achieved through the use of a gusset. The more the front and back overlap, the narrower the leg. Figure 88A: Holly McQuillan; Photographs by Thomas McQuillan. Figure 88B: Holly McQuillan.

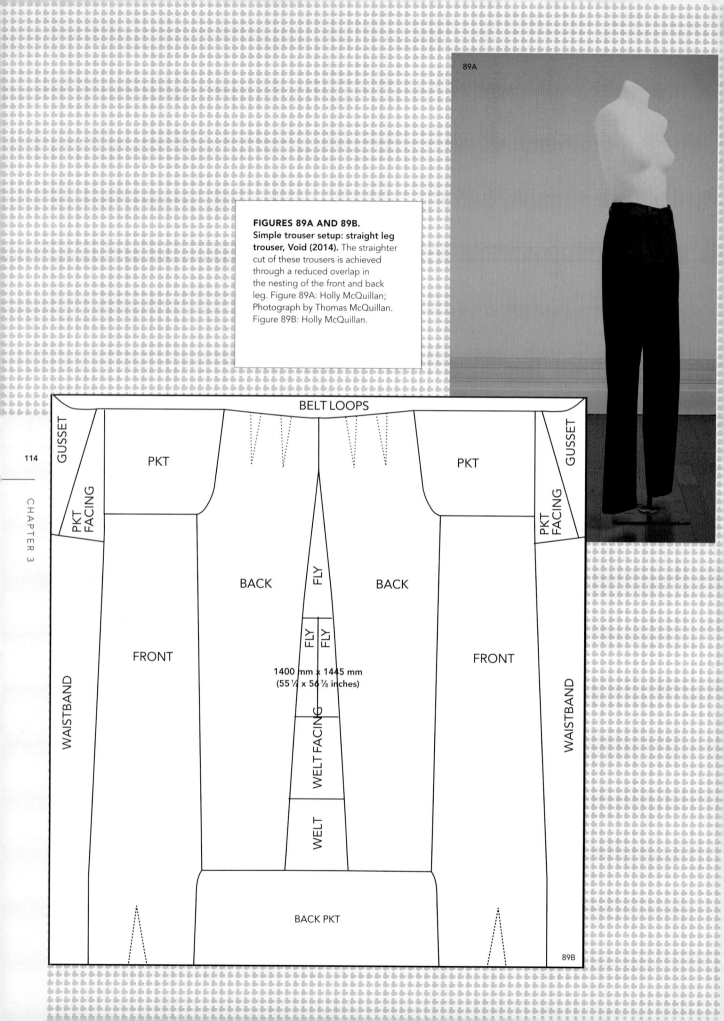

89A

FIGURES 89A AND 89B.
Simple trouser setup: straight leg
trouser, Void (2014). The straighter
cut of these trousers is achieved
through a reduced overlap in
the nesting of the front and back
leg. Figure 89A: Holly McQuillan;
Photograph by Thomas McQuillan.
Figure 89B: Holly McQuillan.

BELT LOOPS

GUSSET

PKT

PKT

GUSSET

PKT FACING

PKT FACING

BACK

FLY

BACK

FLY

FLY

FRONT

1400 mm x 1445 mm
(55 ⅛ x 56 ⅞ inches)

FRONT

WAISTBAND

WELT FACING

WAISTBAND

WELT

BACK PKT

89B

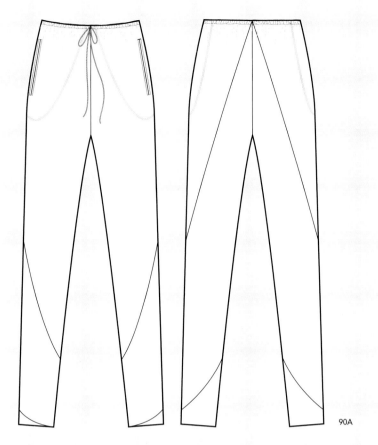

FIGURES 90A AND 90B.
Basic spiral trouser setup: hem width is determined by the difference between fabric width and diagonal line. Leg width is determined by fabric length. Waist and hip width are determined by placement and shape of crotch seam relative to fabric length. This results in a conventional trouser silhouette without side or inseam. Holly McQuillan.

90A

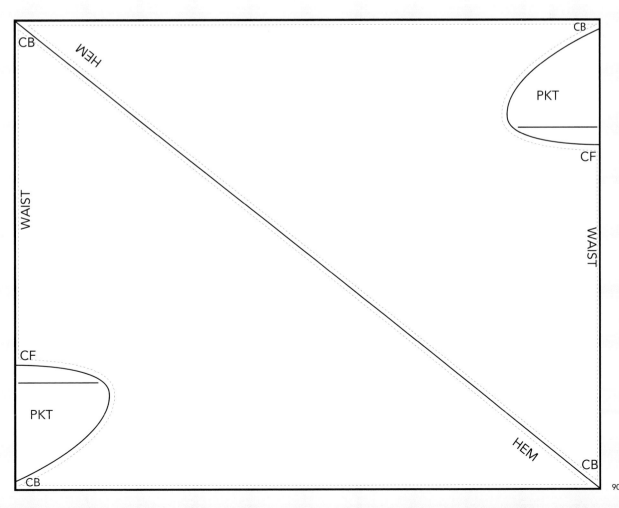

90B

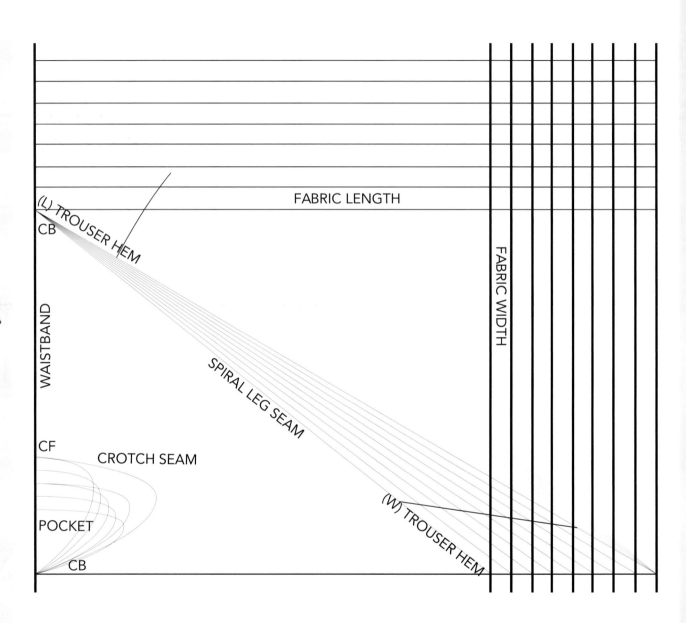

FABRIC LENGTH

FABRIC WIDTH

(L) TROUSER HEM

CB

WAISTBAND

SPIRAL LEG SEAM

CF

CROTCH SEAM

(W) TROUSER HEM

POCKET

CB

91

FIGURE 91.
Spiral trouser matrix showing trouser leg
width/crotch seam/length/taper changes
possible. Holly McQuillan.

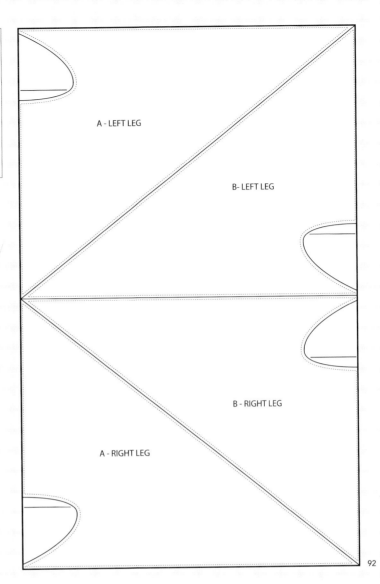

FIGURE 92.
On a cloth with one face, cutting two pairs of spiral trousers together is necessary. Holly McQuillan.

A - LEFT LEG

B- LEFT LEG

B - RIGHT LEG

A - RIGHT LEG

FIGURE 93.
The grain line on the spiral trouser is originally cross grain, but this will only work on particular fabrics. The same basic pattern layout can be adapted for straight grain cutting as shown. Holly McQuillan.

92

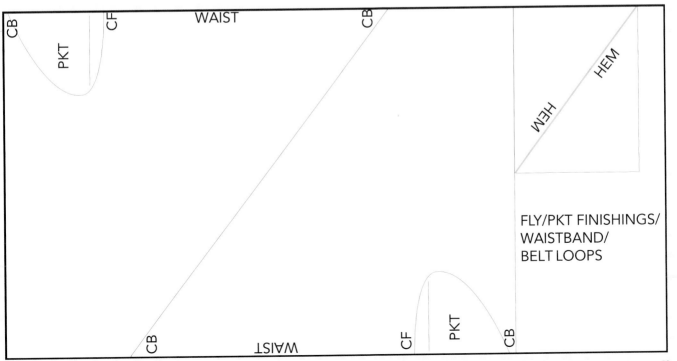

CB

PKT

CF

WAIST

CB

HEM

HEM

FLY/PKT FINISHINGS/ WAISTBAND/ BELT LOOPS

CB

WAIST

CF

PKT

CB

93

TUBE DRESS
Simple geometric cutting

94A

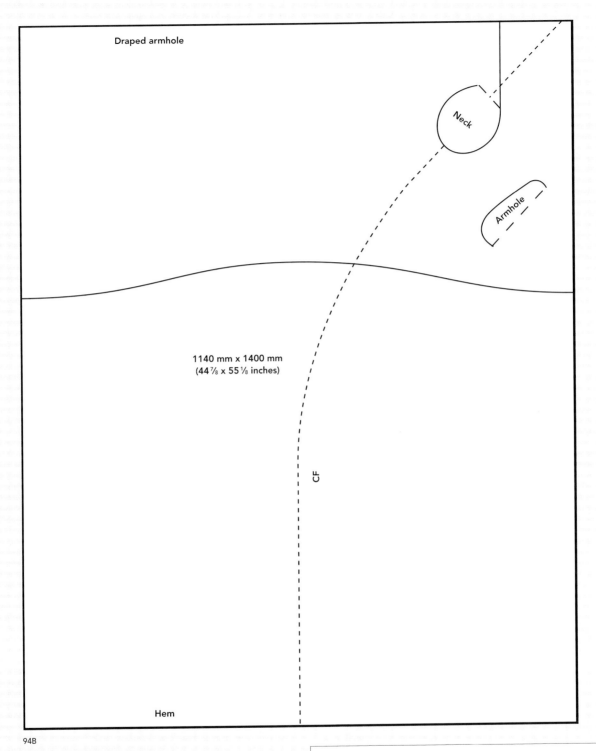

Draped armhole

Neck

Armhole

1140 mm x 1400 mm
(44 7/8 x 55 1/8 inches)

CF

Hem

94B

FIGURES 94A AND 94B.
Tube dress pattern: a single straight seam transforms the flat cloth into a geometric tube for the body to travel through. By offsetting the neckline and armhole, interest is generated through interaction between the cloth and the body. Many variations are possible through adding simple geometric cuts and manipulating the distribution of the cloth around the body. Holly McQuillan.

ADAPTING AN EXISTING DESIGN
FOR ZERO WASTE

Existing designs can be adapted for zero waste. Using a one-piece pattern for the Kimono Twist dress from designer and pattern cutter Anita McAdam of Studio Faro in Sydney, McQuillan attempted to make a zero waste version that maintained the general concept of the original. She used a crisp heavy cotton that was 150 centimeters (59 inches) wide and based the pattern interpretation within those constraints. The design would work well with a knit or softer weave also. The Kimono Twist dress uses negative space as decorative facing, and form support demonstrates how careful pattern design—where particular fit and design feature is required—can lead to a strong solution, which further adds to the silhouette of the garment.

Detailed instructions:

1 Align the center back with the center straight grain of the fabric to create a front extension/collar, akin to the kimono. To accommodate the front twist it is necessary to slash into the new front extension/collar area at the waist.

2 The collar follows around the back of the neck and is taken from the upper shoulder/neck area, to reveal and frame the nape of the neck, similar to a traditional kimono.

3 To save fabric McQuillan divided the back skirt off from the top, and rotated and nested it alongside the front skirt. To do this she straightened the side and center back seams, and put the shaping into two darts, one close to the back side seam and the other in the more usual place for a back dart. The overall placement of the skirt area allows a range of sizes to potentially fit in the basic layout by making the gather/twist or front extension larger or smaller. Also, the skirt length is easily adjusted depending on the preference of the maker/user and potentially the width or length of the fabric you have. Alternately, the front and back can remain as one piece.

4 To further allow for sizing changes, McQuillan ensured the key areas of fit were placed alongside areas where exact shape/size were not as important. In this case the "negative space" is the facing for the front opening, so small changes to the main garment body will not negatively impact the function of the facing.

5 The piece generated from the back kimono sleeve/body is used to make an inseam pocket (McQuillan dislikes dresses without pockets; they seem too formal to her). This piece could also be used to extend the facing for the front if you don't want pockets. Alternately, to remove the pocket, you could make the sleeve wider and come out from the waist. This would change the shape of the facing but will not alter the function of it.

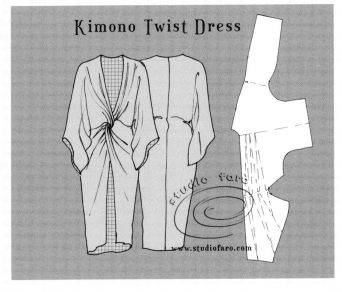

Kimono Twist Dress

studio faro

www.studiofaro.com

95

FIGURE 95.
Original Studio Faro design
for Twist Kimono dress, that
Holly McQuillan adopted for
zero waste. Anita McAdam,
Studio Faro.

FIGURE 96.
Zero waste interpretation of Twist
Kimono design by Holly McQuillan
(2014). The negative space offered by
the existing pattern are used as facings
for the front opening and neckline.
Holly McQuillan.

BACK SKIRT

CB

PKT SLASH

BACK WAIST

COLLAR

FACING

FACING APPLIED

CF

SHOULDER

COLLAR

1500 mm x 1400 mm
(59 1/16 x 55 1/8 inches)

CF

COLLAR

SHOULDER

CB ZIP

BACK WAIST

POCKET

POCKET

BACK SKIRT

CB

PKT SLASH

BACK WAIST

COLLAR

FACING

FACING

96

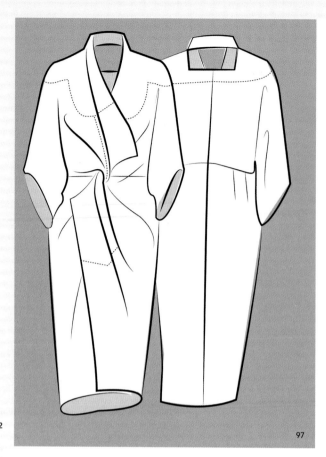

97

FIGURE 97.
Zero waste kimono design by McQuillan. The goal was to maintain the key aesthetic and fit elements of the original design while achieving a zero waste result. Holly McQuillan.

Notes:

The facing acts as finishing and doubles the fabric thickness at the shoulder, therefore supporting the rounded shoulder silhouette if using a semi-rigid cloth. The facing could also be applied to the outside of the garment for a stronger presence.

If your fabric is woven and 140 centimeters (55⅛ inches) wide, you could either narrow the twist and/or extension or (if your fabric allows it) simply rotate the pattern 90 degrees. Other fabric widths can be accommodated by changing the width of the extension and/or amount of twist. You can change the size by widening or narrowing the waistline, by moving where the twist hooks with the other side, and widening/narrowing the corresponding hip/side seam.

McQuillan sewed the garment up primarily using a very narrow rolled hem edge and a lap seaming process for its visual appeal; however, you could use any process you like. The dress has a center-back zipper, which it wouldn't need in a knit.

MCQUILLAN'S REFLECTIONS ON THE KIMONO TWIST DRESS

If I made the pattern square, altering it to suit different fabric widths would be simpler. You can then simply cut a straight section of fabric from selvage to selvage, rotate and sew it somewhere on the straight grain (such as the selvage) of the base fabric to make your fabric the right width. Using this approach the fabric need not be the same, and you could exploit this approach to create a color or texture blocking effect. It also makes widening the pattern for larger sizes easier, as the fabric length poses no constraint in the way the width does. Any square zero waste pattern could be alterable in the manner described above, a useful consideration in an industry context, as it theoretically allows for ease of sizing (grading) and change in fabric width.

RISKY DESIGN PRACTICE

Aakko and Niinimäki (2014: 75) note that "precisely designed forms are . . . challenging" through zero waste fashion design. Practice over time allows unlimited precision in the process. For example, Rissanen was not able to resolve the Endurance shirt to his satisfaction during the making of the Bad Dogs collection in 2007–8. However, he did resolve the shirt's aesthetics, precise fit, and zero waste for the 2009 "Fashioning Now" exhibition. This was due to practice over time and the ability to reflect on past failures and successes. He further refined the shirt in 2011 during "The Cutting Circle" project.

The dominant design ideation tool in conventional fashion design is sketching. The aim is to eliminate uncertainty before patterns are made and fabric is cut. The method is efficient, yet with limitations. A sketch is a proposition and a speculation. Sketching a garment is an effective tool in thinking about its aesthetics—silhouette, color, details. It is not, however, effective in eliminating the fabric waste created when that garment is made. Speculative sketching about how pattern pieces might interact on fabric is useful. Resolving the marker in the final stages requires pattern cutting and marker planning to be adopted alongside conventional design strategies. Within the usual fashion design mindset, this could appear as risky. For example, in early conversations about a particular zero waste design, all the design's visual elements may not be resolved in the same way that they would be in design through sketching. This "risk" may be challenging to embrace. However, openness to possibility during the design process is necessary.

For example, a fabric may become unavailable between sampling and production, which might require swift thinking and action from the designer and the production team. This same dynamic ability to respond to challenges is also essential in zero waste fashion design.

+
Rick Owens on sketching

"Sketches are pretty, but they're too unrealistic. I don't think I ever really sketched. It isn't my thing. One of the reasons is because there's just something too cliché about fashion sketching. I went to art school to be a painter, so I have this standard image that I think is the standard of art, and I think a fashion sketch would be too superficial. And cheap. It just seems corny. It's not a necessary step. It's just like this fantasy. It's like collages. I have this thing against making collages of inspirations and stuff."

http://the-talks.com/interviews/rick-owens/

DESIGNING WITH THE FABRIC WIDTH

In her research into historical cloth and dress, Burnham (1973) pointed out the connection between the loom type used by a particular culture at a particular time, the width of fabric that would result from weaving on that loom, and the kinds of garments that were made from those particular widths. When fashion designers design garments at present day, the width of the fabric is usually not a consideration in the process. Perhaps it should be. It need not be a constraining one; the width is merely the space within which the fashion designer and pattern cutter have the conversation about the design being developed. The fabric width is an intrinsic quality of the fabric, which in turn is the primary material that fashion designers work with. The width can be the source of design ideas, and conversations about it and within it can bridge gaps between fashion design and fashion manufacturing.

Fabrics come in many different widths and various strategies exist within zero waste fashion design to respond to new widths dynamically and quickly. Fabric width, while perhaps a new consideration for many fashion designers, can be an opportunity in design, when approached creatively.

98

FIGURE 98.
The geometric maxi dress is made by piecing two shades of gray fabric together to create new fabric widths and colorways.
Holly McQuillan.

99A

99B

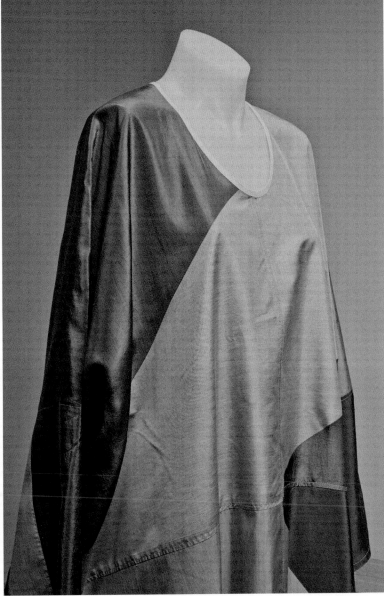

99C

FIGURES 99A, 99B, AND 99C.
The geometric maxi dress is made
by piecing two shades of gray fabric
together to create new fabric widths
and colorways. Holly McQuillan;
Photographs by Thomas McQuillan.

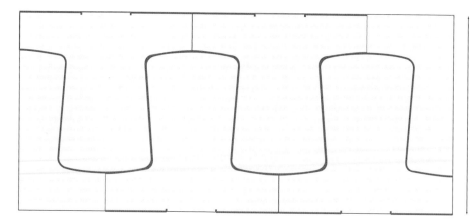

Width of fabric determines dress length
In this case the width of the fabric is 115cm

□ Two layers of polyester

—— Red lines to be laser cut

▬▬ Thicker blue lines
to be laser seamed

100A

FIGURES 100A AND 100B.
Dress designed collaboratively by
Dr. Kate Goldsworthy and David Telfer.
The design is adaptable to various fabric
widths; the fabric width determines the
dress length. Kate Goldsworthy.

100B

SHORT CUTS

1 Examining Donella Meadows's places to intervene in a fashion system (Fletcher 2014: 71–85), could zero waste fashion design facilitate systemic change in fashion, and how?

2 Choose instructions for one garment in the chapter to prototype, and document the prototyping process. How would you redesign the garment?

3 Having completed the prototype, reflect on the design opportunities presented by different fabric widths for the same garment.

zero waste fashion design and CAD

Certain phases of the zero waste fashion design process can become easier and faster with the help of digital technologies, here referred to as computer-aided design (CAD). It may be obvious that CAD systems for pattern cutting and marker making can be useful. However, systems not originally intended for pattern cutting, such as Adobe Illustrator, can also be harnessed for zero waste fashion design. Any technology is as good as the person using it, and practice over time is key.

MARKER MAKING AS DESIGN ACTIVITY

So far the discussion has contextualized pattern cutting as designing, but in zero waste fashion design marker making is also an integral part of design activity. Conventionally the process of marker making occurs after design and pattern cutting, often by someone far removed from the designer or pattern cutter, resulting in oddly shaped spaces between pieces, which are often unusable. However, by understanding marker making as a design activity, the opportunities for design and waste reduction and elimination are boundless. At its simplest, this approach means pocket bag shapes can be modified to better use more available space; at its most complex, multiple garments can be designed simultaneously, not in reaction to the negative space, but as though there was never any negative space to begin with. This process, when supported by digital methods, can yield even greater and more flexible results.

The use of digital technology to develop zero waste patterns is by no means necessary—every designer works differently and within the different resources available. The imperative thing is to find a way that works well for the individual and the company.

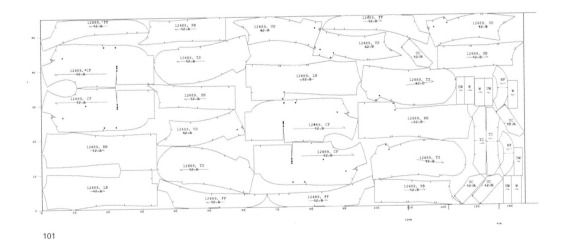

101

FIGURE 101.
Marker of a conventional jacket showing fabric wastage.
Kathleen Fasanella.

ADVANTAGES OF DIGITAL DESIGN FOR ZERO WASTE FASHION

Using digital means to develop and resolve a zero waste garment can solve a number of challenges that a practitioner is likely to encounter. It is an obvious solution to the large-scale patterns that zero waste fashion design may produce, especially in the developmental stage. Because you are essentially working with a marker through most of the process, working in half-scale or digitally can both be useful solutions. Additionally, working digitally enables the designer to print small-scale paper patterns to test out the basic arrangement of pattern pieces as a means of developing the design without cutting and potentially wasting large sections of cloth. Blocks can easily be copied and dissected into pieces when needed, and you can switch easily between working in full-scale and half-scale, changing the fabric width and length with little effort. Other advantages include the easy integration of other digital methods into the design process, such as digital print design, and the portability of a digital file, either for personal use or to send digitally anywhere. Once you understand the process and limitations of CAD methods, they can enable the easy development of zero waste garments in both their entirety or as one part of a larger design development process.

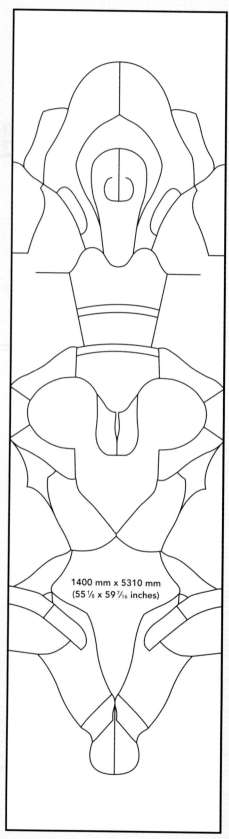

1400 mm x 5310 mm
(55 1/8 x 59 7/16 inches)

FIGURE 102.
Twinset pattern: this pattern is over 5 meters long and makes three different garments: a reversible dress, a top, and a pair of slim-fitting trousers. Holly McQuillan.

102

103A

103B

ZERO WASTE TUTORIALS THROUGH CAD

CAD systems with pattern cutting and marker-making capability include Gerber, Lectra, OptiTex, and StyleCAD. In the absence of these systems, Adobe Illustrator and other vector graphics software can also be used as design tools. Additionally, as with any tool, you are not required to use a system for its exact purpose or only utilize methods explained in the instructions. Experiment, push boundaries, and use combinations of technology and manual methods. Play and find the way of working that works best for you. As such, the following step-by-step guides should only be used as a starting point and are only directly applicable for the specific software described. They are merely tools and imperfect tools at that; however, they are effective catalysts for getting started with a zero waste garment.

MCQUILLAN ON ADOBE ILLUSTRATOR + ACCUMARK GERBER FOR ZERO WASTE

When working digitally I use a combination of Illustrator and Gerber. I primarily use Gerber for generating conventional blocks: exporting them as .dxf files to import into Illustrator and for printing off full-scale and half-scale zero waste patterns when testing the patterns. I use Adobe Illustrator (Tip Box 1) to develop the zero waste pattern itself, and I print small-scale test patterns (on A4 or A3 paper) to cut and assemble with tape to check basic pattern piece use and the resulting silhouette. This is kind of three-dimensional design development sketching.

TIP 1

Download Inkscape for free if you don't have Illustrator (http://www.inkscape.org).

TIP 2

DFX files are transferable between digital mediums such as Gerber and Illustrator. Import .dxf files into Illustrator, Inkscape, or whichever software you are using.

TIP 3

Adding seam allowances in Illustrator:

Select the line you want to add seam allowance to, using the Selection Tool. Copy and paste in front (ctrl c > ctrl f). Effect > Path > Offset Path. Put in the seam size you're wanting (1 centimeter/ 10 millimeters/ ⅜ inch, for example). Press return/ ok, then click Object > Expand appearance.

If the line is closed (like an O) then it will add the seam allowance on the outside. If the line is open (like a C) it will go around the inside and outside of the line/curve. Once you click "Expand appearance," you can edit or delete the parts you don't want.

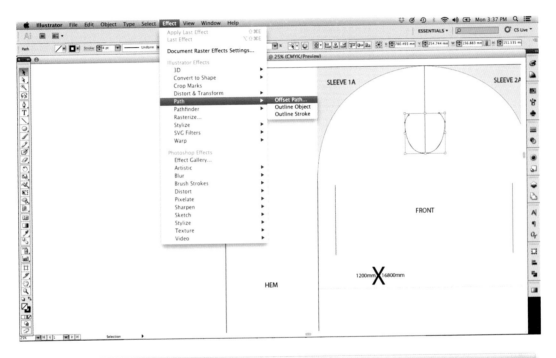

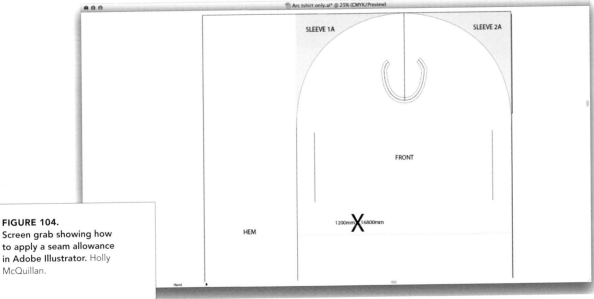

FIGURE 104.
Screen grab showing how to apply a seam allowance in Adobe Illustrator. Holly McQuillan.

TIP 4

Basic Illustrator functions for pattern making:

Copy:	Reflect:	Divide block/pieces:	Rotate:
Select pattern piece	Select pattern piece	Use pen tool to draw a dividing line over closed pattern piece	Select pattern piece
▼	▼	▼	▼
ctrl c	right click	Select both dividing line and pattern piece	Rotate Tool (R)
▼	▼	▼	▼
ctrl f or v	transform	Pathfinder palette (divide)	move rotational point to desired pivoting point on pattern
	▼	▼	▼
	reflect	right click	click and drag pattern piece around to desired position
		▼	
		ungroup	

1 Block choice (garment type—for example, trousers, jacket, skirt, etc.): Select the block type you want to use based on the garment type and size you are aiming for. You can scan half-scale patterns and trace over them in Illustrator, or alternately you can use systems like OptiTex or Gerber to generate digital blocks. Export the block as a .dxf file (Tip Box 2). McQuillan uses blocks without seam allowances and adds them as needed (Tip Box 3).

2 Choose your fabric and measure its exact width; this is the space within which you design. In many designs there is some flexibility in relation to the fabric width; you can move things around a bit and the general design remains pretty much the same.

3 Set up the Artboard as your "fabric," as it is easy to extend the length almost indefinitely. Choose whether you would like to work full-scale or half-scale. Both work equally well, and you can alternate between scales without any problems. Your Artboard width should be your fabric width, and the height is your length. Note: you choose what orientation you use. McQuillan's pattern making lecturer always instructed, "Hems to the left!" but in Illustrator she does not follow his probably good advice!

4 Fabric = Artboard: Start with the width of the fabric: 1.5 to 2 meters (roughly 1.5 to 2 yards) long. You can always make it shorter or longer as your design progresses. The area surrounding the Artboard can be used as a "waiting room" for pattern pieces not yet used and a sketch pad for layout ideas (much like a table surface if you were pattern cutting manually). This area will not print, but it will be saved with the file for future reference.

5 Layers: Use layers to ease navigation through the file. You need a layer for blocks, another for cut lines, and another for labels would be the minimum needed.

6 Importing blocks: File > Place > Block_Name.ai The block will be full-scale, so if your Illustrator file is set up as half-scale you'll need to select the block > right click > transform > scale > 50%.

7 Planning your design's "fixed areas." What parts of the final garment do you want to fit the body in a particular manner? Do you need to pattern cut these in a conventional manner first? These form the foundation of your design, and they could be as extensive or minimal as you like. Bear in mind that the more fixed areas you have and the more rigid you are in the application of these, the less flexible the design process becomes. For example, you could start with the shoulder areas as the only fixed areas for a more flexible design process.

Sizing should be considered here; see Chapter 5 on sizing, as well as the section on grading in this chapter.

8 Design: Place the blocks and pattern pieces needed for any fixed areas on the Artboard so that the negative space—the spaces between the pattern pieces—begin to form pleasing shapes. Consider the placement of fixed areas next to those where the exact size and shape is less important. Shapes such as teardrops and curves work well, as do straight sections that you can easily incorporate into other garment parts or functions (pockets, facings, etc.). McQuillan avoids using decoration as a means of disposing of the waste. She prefers a "macro" approach to zero waste pattern cutting, but this depends on your overall design aesthetic: if embellishment is your thing, go for it.

9 Move the blocks, slash and spread them, create new design lines, extending the length of fabric if and where required, until you have utilized the entire fabric width, and however long the length ends up being.

10 At this point it can be useful to print out the pattern on A4 paper, cut it out, and stick it together with tape to do an initial test of the overall design and to see if everything will fit and be used as planned. Make any alterations as needed.

11 Export an Adobe Illustrator (.ai) file at .dxf. Import using Data Conversion Utility in Accumark (see Tip 2). Print from Gerber as a single pattern piece. Make a toile in half-scale if you have a half-scale mannequin, using the paper model as a guide. Remember that a half-scale toile will not behave exactly as full-scale but nonetheless provides a credible indication of the garment in full-scale. Make alterations as needed. Sew up the final garment using the half-scale version as a guide.

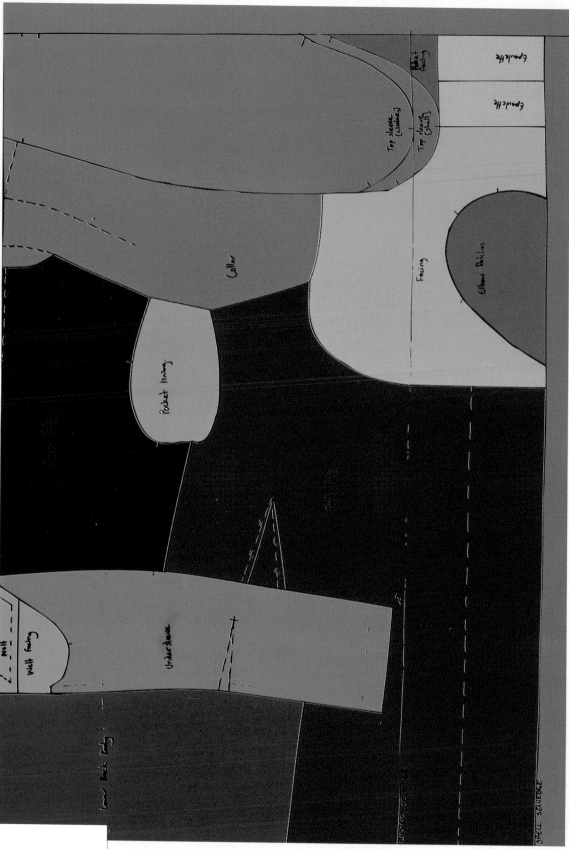

FIGURE 105.
Using color coding to help
with pattern development.
Holly McQuillan.

The design can be symmetrical or not—sometimes parts are set up as symmetrical and others are not as this can help the overall layout and final garment design.

Remember that in zero waste fashion design every line you design on your pattern has two sides. You are designing both sides of the line and will use the fabric on both sides of the scissors when you sew it up.

Think about how the chosen fabric might behave when sewn up in the shapes you make. Remember that any shape will sew into any void so long as the circumference is the same (thanks to Julian Roberts).

Remember that fabric is soft and is affected by gravity—it will hang from points on the body.

Pay particular attention to seams (Tip Box 3), particularly for areas such as sleeve crowns/caps and armholes, where fit is extremely important. In many areas seam allowances are less important. Use your common sense to work out where it is important (usually where things will fit closely to the figure).

Using color to code the sections can help (e.g., sleeves in yellow, body in red, etc.).

GRADING AND CAD

Conventional grading of a garment pattern occurs after the design and pattern cutting processes are complete. It is not possible to grade a zero waste garment in a conventional manner if the intention is that all sizes are zero waste. The smaller and larger pattern pieces of the graded sizes will not interlock in the same manner as the original sample size. It is therefore important to consider this goal from the outset,

when developing a zero waste garment, if the intention is to make it available in a range of sizes. When embedding multiple sizes into a zero waste pattern, McQuillan often begins with the graded nest of sizes generated by a CAD system that provides a clear visual to guide the placement of fixed areas (pertinent to fit) next to flexible areas of the pattern. This is discussed further in Chapter 5.

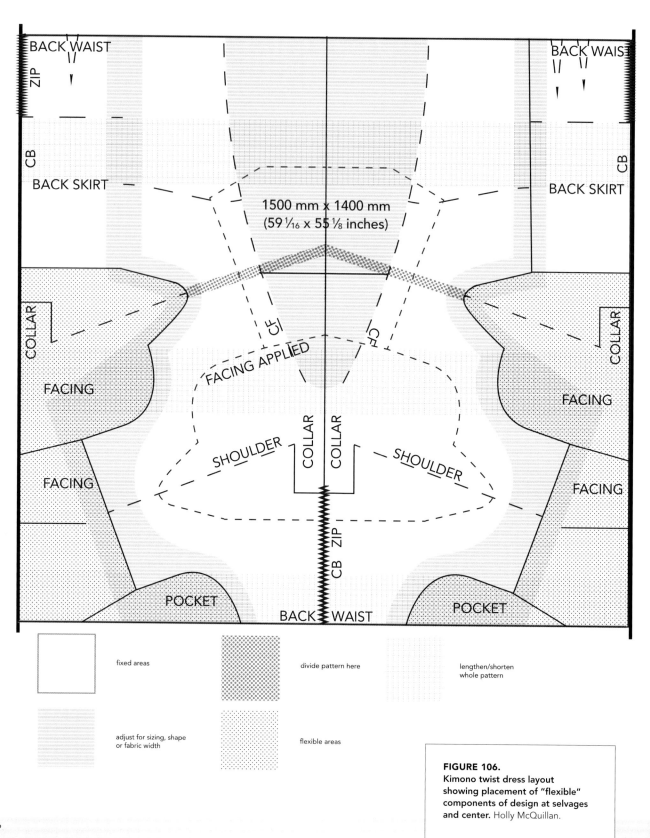

BACK WAIST

ZIP

CB

BACK SKIRT

1500 mm x 1400 mm
(59 1/16 x 55 1/8 inches)

BACK WAIST

CB

BACK SKIRT

COLLAR

FACING

FACING

FACING APPLIED

CF

CF

SHOULDER

COLLAR

COLLAR

SHOULDER

COLLAR

FACING

FACING

POCKET

CB ZIP

POCKET

BACK WAIST

| | fixed areas | | divide pattern here | | lengthen/shorten whole pattern |
| | adjust for sizing, shape or fabric width | | flexible areas | | |

FIGURE 106.
Kimono twist dress layout showing placement of "flexible" components of design at selvages and center. Holly McQuillan.

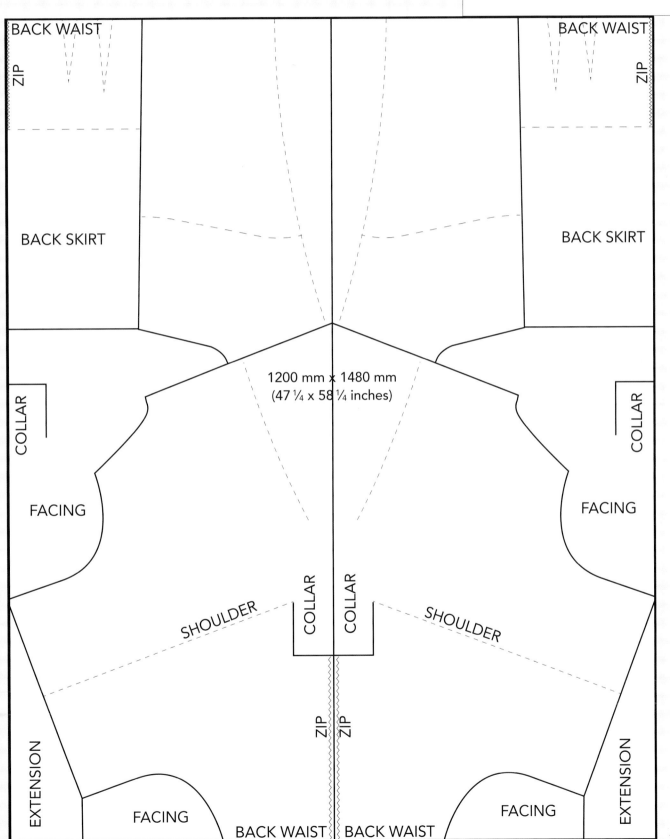

FIGURE 107.
The 120-centimeter-wide version of the kimono pattern maintains the fundamental form, fit, and details of the original design. Holly McQuillan.

BACK WAIST

ZIP

BACK WAIST

ZIP

BACK SKIRT

BACK SKIRT

1200 mm x 1480 mm
(47 ¼ x 58 ¼ inches)

COLLAR

COLLAR

FACING

FACING

COLLAR

COLLAR

SHOULDER

SHOULDER

ZIP

ZIP

EXTENSION

EXTENSION

FACING

FACING

BACK WAIST

BACK WAIST

107

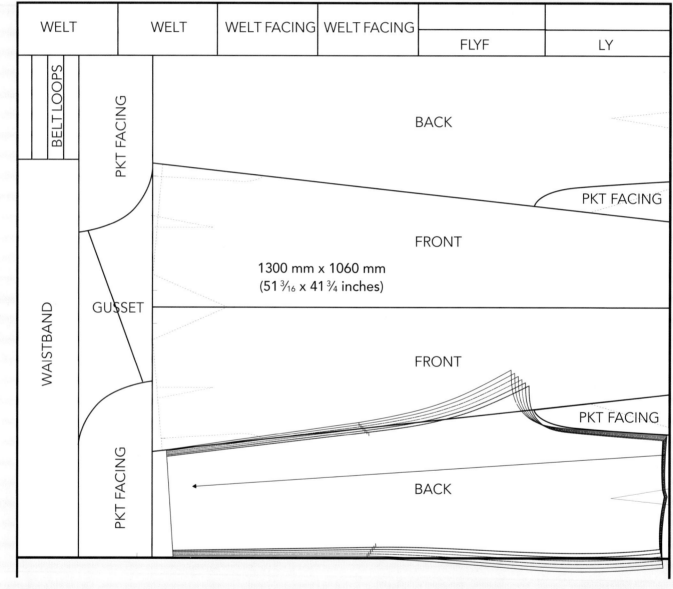

Within the figure:

| WELT | WELT | WELT FACING | WELT FACING | | |
| | | | | FLYF | LY |

BELT LOOPS

PKT FACING

WAISTBAND

GUSSET

PKT FACING

BACK

PKT FACING

FRONT

1300 mm x 1060 mm
(51 3/16 x 41 3/4 inches)

FRONT

PKT FACING

BACK

108

FIGURE 108.
Graded nest used to develop zero
waste trouser pattern; growth in
trouser width for each size can be
accommodated by lengthening the
fabric piece used. Holly McQuillan.

COMBINING DIGITAL TECHNOLOGIES

A key advantage of digital pattern cutting in fashion design (whether zero waste or not) is the ease of combining it with other digital technologies, such as laser cutting, digital textile print, and digital embroidery. Laser cutting zero waste patterns allows for accurate cutting of pieces where each cut has two sides. Zero waste pattern design can result in unusual pattern shapes that require greater consideration of construction techniques; however, the use of synthetic fabric (polyester, nylon) combined with the use of heat-sealed edges, or the use of digital embroidery to finish difficult pattern shapes, can potentially mitigate this, while adding to the aesthetic of the garment. Digital textile printing allows the application of the garment pieces and textile pattern onto the fabric surface simultaneously.

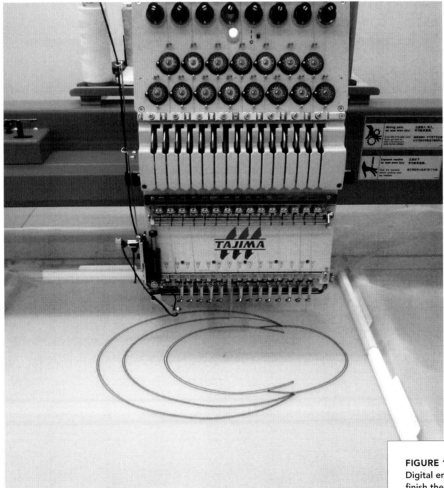

FIGURE 109.
Digital embroidery can be used to finish the edges of garment when traditional finishing is difficult.
Greta Menzies.

ZERO WASTE AND DIGITAL TEXTILE DESIGN

Twinset is a collaborative fashion/textile design that was developed through research at the intersections of digital textile design and zero waste fashion design. Through an iterative process of exchange and response, the design evolved out of the junctions between Holly McQuillan's zero waste fashion research and Genevieve Packer's digital textile print exploration.

Twinset embeds a dress, vest, and pant into a single zero waste pattern, exploring the opportunities that embedding multiple garments in a single pattern reveals and the advantages that digital printing lends to this approach. The garments appear to be made from very different fabrics but in fact are all produced from the same piece of cloth. This approach gives greater flexibility for zero waste fashion design by enabling more control of the process while ensuring consumers are provided choice in a sustainable manner.

The starting point is the slim fitting trouser, using curved panels and cut on the bias for ease of movement. These were pattern cut in a traditional manner, using a digital pattern to achieve the desired slim aesthetic. The pieces for the trouser were laid out on the cloth to create negative spaces that became the dress and vest. This approach enables a degree of control in parts of a design and embraces the fluidity of McQuillan's design process for the other garments, enabling balance between fit and fullness, tradition and innovation.

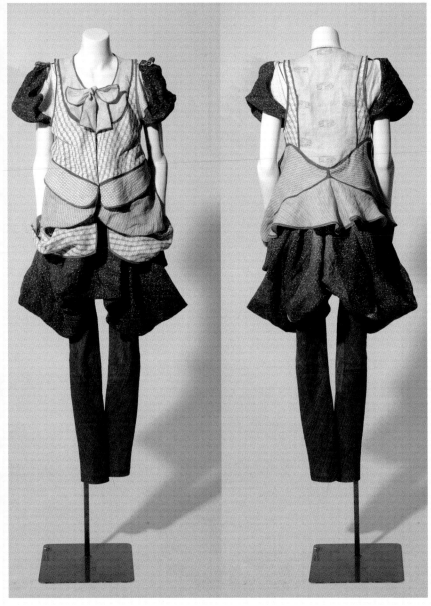

111A

111B

FIGURE 110.
Digital textile printing allows a single zero waste pattern to provide for the appearance of different fabrics and colors. **Holly McQuillan collaborated on this 100% linen design with New Zealand textile designer Genevieve Packer.** Genevieve Packer; Holly McQuillan.

FIGURES 111A AND 111B.
Each of the three garments were made from the same digitally printed textile pattern. The print has been engineered to fit both the 3D garment design and the 2D zero waste pattern. Photographs by Thomas McQuillan.

INTERVIEW WITH JULIA LUMSDEN

Julia Lumsden is a New Zealand fashion designer who completed her Master of Design at Massey University exploring the use of CAD software (specifically Gerber Accumark) for zero waste men's garment design.

+ **Can you tell us a little about your background and how you came to study fashion design?**

I grew up in Hamilton, New Zealand, and loved all kinds of craft from a young age—I started making hand-stitched teddy bears at age seven. I first had regular access to a sewing machine at high school, in Textiles (a class), where I learned about various textile crafts and dressmaking using domestic sewing patterns. I would design by combining elements from various home sew patterns. While I was good academically all round, Textiles was what I loved and excelled at. I was motivated to apply for the bachelor of design (BDes) at Massey University, Wellington, as the four-year degree format seemed to provide an outlet for my passion for sewing while at the same time providing an academic challenge.

+ **When did you begin exploring (what could be considered) zero waste fashion? What was your motivation to begin designing this way?**

In the final year of my undergraduate degree, I completed an independent study paper in which I researched the alterations function of the Gerber pattern design software. Through this research I developed a way of using it as a design tool. The alterations menu is conventionally used to alter an existing pattern to fit an individual's measurements, a process that is sometimes referred to as "Made to Measure." The way I chose to test this program as a design tool was to use the same function to alter the pattern so that I achieved the best possible yield, which I termed "Made to Measure, for the Cloth." I tested the process out on a men's jacket pattern and achieved an aesthetically pleasing result with a yield of 93 percent. I continued experimenting with this process while developing the idea and producing designs for my final collection and fully developed five more jacket patterns. In the marker stage, the patterns had a yield of between 93 percent and 97 percent but, by taking the development of the patterns one step further, these jackets all had a yield of 100 percent.

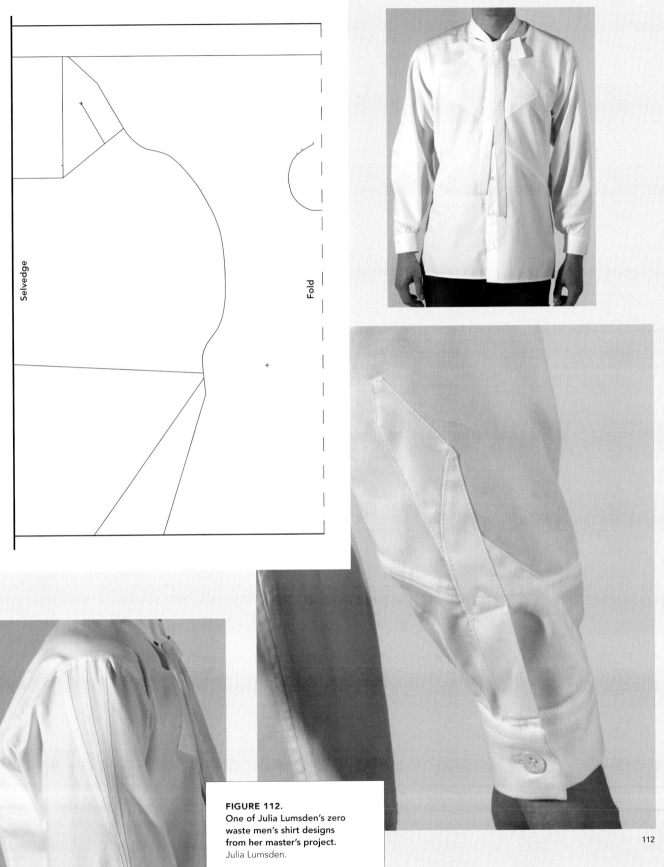

Selvedge

Fold

FIGURE 112.
One of Julia Lumsden's zero
waste men's shirt designs
from her master's project.
Julia Lumsden.

112

I transformed the pattern manipulation process into a method of design creation. It was through manipulation of the pattern to achieve the best possible yield that the jackets took on a unique design aesthetic.

+ **What about the relationship between CAD (in your case Gerber software) and zero waste design—did working within these parameters challenge you/excite you?**

The choice to use CAD came first. I learned the basics of pattern making through flat pattern making and then was introduced to CAD. I continued to use both CAD and flat pattern making throughout my degree; however, once introduced to it, I immediately had a preference for CAD. My reasons are largely practical; the speed, accuracy, and tidy containment of digital storage all appealed to me. I came to zero waste design because of my preference for CAD pattern making. It seemed to me that zero waste design was a complementary expression of the efficiency, accuracy, and transformability offered by CAD.

One of the main parameters during my master's was to stay true to my minimalist tailored menswear with quirky details design aesthetic. The transformations applied in CAD to get to a zero waste pattern were a rich source of the quirky detailing that was integral to my design aesthetic, and this is what made the design process exciting for me.

+ **What do you think the industry might be able to learn from the work you've done in your BDes and master's?**

Through my master's thesis, I was interested in exploring whether design through CAD, using zero waste as a design parameter, could be successful in creating structured, tailored menswear. Through my thesis, I developed a series of techniques that could be applied to a regular block that could create a zero waste pattern for a structured garment, in this case the shirt. As an example, a technique called "piecing" involved chopping up larger pattern pieces, which allowed them to be arranged more efficiently on the fabric. This would create new design lines that would add aesthetic interest to the garment. This technique worked well, as it required minimal distortion of the original block. However, with this process, the issue of sizing and grading became more apparent; in order to make different grades, I would essentially need to return to the original block, grade the block, and then reapply the zero waste techniques. This is an area that could potentially be optimized through CAD.

This work led me to question the wider issue of sustainability within the fashion industry. For me, bespoke tailoring is the future of sustainable fashion design, making garments that people want and that fit them perfectly rather than mass-producing garments that aren't quite right and may never be worn. CAD has huge potential to make bespoke pattern making and tailoring much more efficient.

+ **Do you have any advice for someone wanting to begin exploring the intersection of zero waste fashion and CAD software?**

CAD is an amazing and essentially limitless design tool for people looking at developing zero waste design techniques. Go into designing using CAD with an open mind, without too many preconceived ideas of what the end result might look like, and give yourself some clear design parameters to help focus your work.

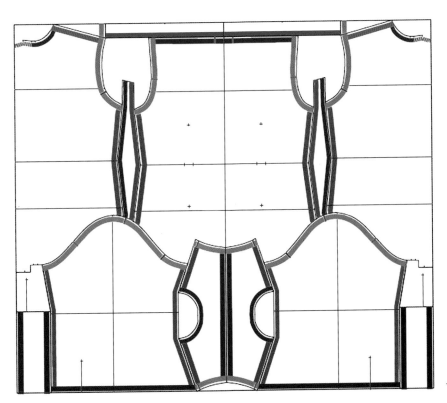

113

FIGURE 113.
Lumsden's shirt design utilizing digital textile printing. Julia Lumsden.

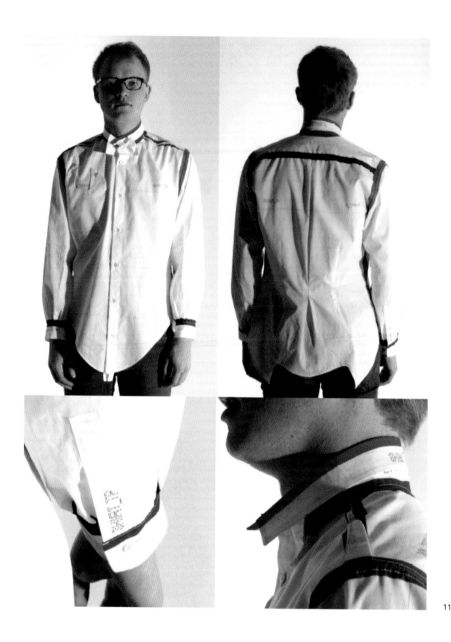

114

FIGURE 114.
Lumsden's shirt design utilizing digital textile printing to illustrate where each piece connects to the other to construct the garment. Issues with shrinkage became apparent (see collar) so this needs to be considered if using digital print processes. Julia Lumsden.

SHORT CUTS

1 Consider your own design practice and skill set: how do you best harness your existing expertise for zero waste fashion design?

2 Do the pattern tutorial in this chapter, either using Adobe Illustrator or Inkscape (open source and free). What opportunities open up for fashion design from this exercise?

3 How could technologies like laser cutting and digital embroidery enrich your zero waste design practice?

manufacturing zero waste garments

Zero waste fashion design can be a catalyst for forging a closer relationship between fashion design and fashion manufacture. When designers begin to consider eliminating fabric waste, new challenges arise from the existing fashion system. This chapter examines those challenges, with the intention to frame them as opportunities for reimagining the entire system of fashion. For example, the practices around creating ranges of sizes of garments require rethinking for zero waste fashion design. Fabric, the material of fashion, also poses challenges for fashion design if the intention is not to waste any of it.

FIGURE 115.
In Deb Cumming and Nina Weaver's dress
the perforations that are laser cut into the
wool felt cloth allow the otherwise stiff fabric
to drape more fluidly. Deb Cumming.

116A

FIGURES 116A AND 116B.
Deb Cumming and Nina Weaver's
laser cut, felted wool dress utilizes
innovative pattern cutting and
construction techniques to develop
a one-piece garment that requires
minimal sewing to wear. Deb Cumming.

116B

FASHION DESIGN AND FASHION MANUFACTURING

Research has demonstrated that within zero waste fashion design certain practices that traditionally reside in manufacturing, such as grading and marker making, are integral to design. Zero waste fashion design could facilitate transformation in the hierarchies that exist in the fashion system, with possible positive implications for both design and manufacturing.

The hierarchical division of labor in fashion design and manufacturing has its roots in practices established by Charles Frederick Worth in the late nineteenth century (de Marly 1980: 22). Worth was the first fashion designer in the modern sense, establishing the role as a predominantly creative profession (Rennolds Milbank 1985: 24–36). Although Worth worked exclusively within haute couture, the fashion designer at the top of the fashion hierarchy is equally applicable in ready-to-wear.

Fletcher (2014: 222–223) argues that the myth of the genius designer has negative implications for consumers' perception of their own skills and knowledge relating to garment alteration and maintenance. Those implications may extend to the roles in the hierarchy, in the sense that the designer's view may receive disproportionate weight. In zero waste fashion design that would not work, as the expertise of each is nonnegotiable to the success of the whole.

Zero waste fashion design could be a catalyst for the reorganization of the hierarchy, because a close, engaged relationship between design and manufacturing is required. Roles traditionally separated from design—pattern cutting, grading, and marker planning and making—all become indispensable components of fashion design. Zero waste fashion design includes pattern cutting as a practice of design. With manufacturing, the scope of design (including pattern cutting) expands to grading and marker making.

FIGURE 117.
Anke Gruendel is a fashion designer, pattern cutter, and a teacher at Parsons. Here she is wearing a zero waste top she designed. The top can be worn three different ways. Anke Gruendel; Photograph by Timo Rissanen.

117

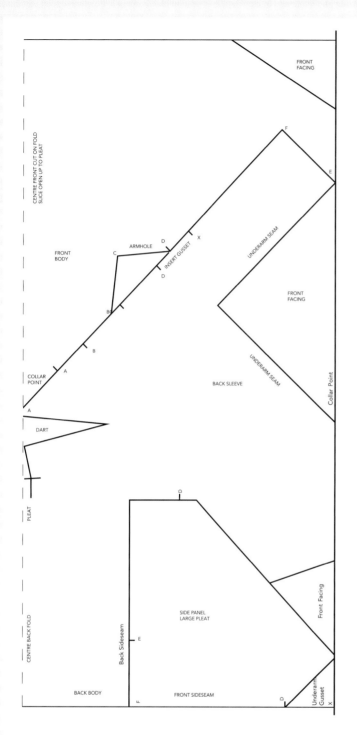

FIGURE 118.
Anke Gruendel's pattern
demonstrates that cutting on
the bias need not be wasteful.
Pleating and darting create a
refined fit in a geometrically cut
garment. Anke Gruendel.

This is not to suggest that the roles should merge to one, potentially eliminating one or more of these sources of employment. Rather, the kinds of communications that occur between these roles could be transformed. In zero waste fashion design and manufacturing, the pattern cutter, pattern grader, and marker planner and maker need to be an integral part of the design process. While this sounds like a simple proposition, the current hierarchies and consequent structures in industry pose formidable challenges for this. For example, with offshore manufacturing the pattern grader and marker planner are likely to be in a different physical location from the designer and pattern cutter; in some instances, the pattern cutter may be offshore as well.

Perhaps the greatest challenge to transforming the industry is the traditional elevation of fashion design above the rest of the industry roles. Fletcher & Grose (2012: 157–179) and Fry (2009: 41–103) present entirely new opportunities for design, including new ways of engaging, not just with the rest of the industry, but also with humanity in its entirety.

INTERVIEW WITH LELA JACOBS

Lela Jacobs is a self-trained New Zealand fashion designer and owner of "The Keep," an open fashion studio and retail space. Her work is minimal and understated with an emphasis on strong design, innovation, and androgynous forms. She works closely with the local New Zealand maker community, collaborating with artists, weavers, knitters, and printers to produce her collections.

Visit Lela's website here: www.lelajacobs.co.nz

+ **Can you tell us a little about your background and how you came to be a fashion designer?**

I was born to a farmer and a city girl in 1980, living rurally on farms around New Zealand until the age of ten when my parents separated and my two sisters and I ventured into the cities with Mum. I have lived all over the country, and when asked where I'm from, the best response for me is simply New Zealand. From as young as I could remember I have always been using my parents' maker tools. As both of them made most things we needed growing up, I learned how to be self-sufficient in these terms from them. Consequently, I don't need much to keep me happy apart from a studio and tools to make with.

I have always felt a little uncomfortable about the title of the fashion designer, as I'm a self-taught maker and oppose fast fashion trends. My design philosophies are centered by responses to people's needs, changing and evolving with what science, community, and environments bring. I also strive to build things that won't cause guilty impacts on an increasingly damaged, sensitive planet. I like to feel this is a positive, essential aspect that should be found in all contemporary designers' ego.

+ **Some of your work is zero waste (or very close to it). What is it about the process of designing in this way that appeals to you?**

In my early twenties, I started folding cloth and cutting into it rather than cutting out of it. This was both really fun and successful for me. At the time this new method had little to do with zero waste and its environmental benefits. It was more about pushing design traditions around and experimentation. Now older and, in some respects, wiser, I can appreciate the rule of zero waste as a design motivation.

CHAPTER 5

FIGURE 119.
Garment by Lela Jacobs.
Lela Jacobs is a New Zealand designer who explores minimal and zero waste design within her ranges (see interview on pp. 155, 157). Lela Jacobs.

+ Is there a reason you don't use zero waste as a marketing tool?

When people come into my open studio and I feel they are or would be interested in zero waste patterns, I will talk with them about it and perhaps even show them how to make some if they are a maker and their energy is worth investing in. I have a history of making freely available, or open sourcing if you like, designs from my collections. Home Sewn by the New Zealand Fashion Museum includes some of these patterns. With regards to promoting it, it's possible subconsciously I was waiting for you to celebrate this with, as there aren't a lot of us doing it, and I don't want to come across like I'm doing this great environmentally friendly process for money. It takes the right exposure to ensure the reasons behind design decisions are conveyed honestly.

+ Many users of this book will be students. Is there any advice you can give them when designing garments with minimal or no waste?

I have always worked closely with the cloth, and I think in order to achieve zero waste and come up with something interesting you're better to work backward and let your cloth design for you. You will be inherently restricted by cloth width, drape, weft and warp, and bias so there is a need to open your mind and take risks, experiment, as it's hard to know how things will fall on the body until they do. Please remember nothing is finished, so don't try and finish the design on paper or in your head. Let it evolve and pay special attention to detail, cloth choice, and finishings. Some eyes see everything!

FIGURE 120.
Garment by Lela Jacobs. The voluminous and androgenous aesthetic of her line lends itself easily to zero waste fashion design processes. Lela Jacobs.

120

SIZING ZERO WASTE GARMENTS

Grading is the process of increasing and decreasing the size of the original pattern to create a range of sizes while keeping the design unchanged. To retain the integrity of the design, it is advisable to keep the size range of a garment design to five or fewer (Fasanella 1998: 170–1). Grading emerged with ready-to-wear clothing to ensure that a range of consumers across sizes would be catered to. Grading is done once there are confirmed orders for the garment style and the style and its patterns have been approved. While pattern cutters are generally trained in manual or digital grading, there are also pattern graders who specialize in grading but not necessarily pattern cutting. Nesting refers to having all of the sizes overlaid with each other.

Grading patterns may seem challenging in the context of zero waste fashion design. The garment components have been designed to configure on a fabric width so that no fabric is wasted. There is no space between the components for them to grow, and if they shrink, gaps would appear. Many components increase or decrease in size horizontally in the direction of the warp grain and vertically in the direction of the weft grain. Generally the largest relative change occurs horizontally in chest, waist, and hip circumference. Vertical change is relatively less, and it is easily addressed; a larger size would simply require a longer length of fabric. Horizontal change is more challenging; as the garment components grow, their overall configuration will expand beyond the width of the fabric.

Similarly, with a smaller size, as the components become smaller, spaces emerge between them on fabric, creating fabric waste. However, these challenges arise from the assumptions that the overall configuration of the garment components, the marker, remains unchanged, and that the conventional rules and methods of grading are used. These need not be the case.

Five possible pathways to creating a range of sizes of a zero waste garment:

1 One-size-fits-most

2 Conventional grading

3 Designing each size individually

4 Using a different fabric width for each size

5 A hybrid method

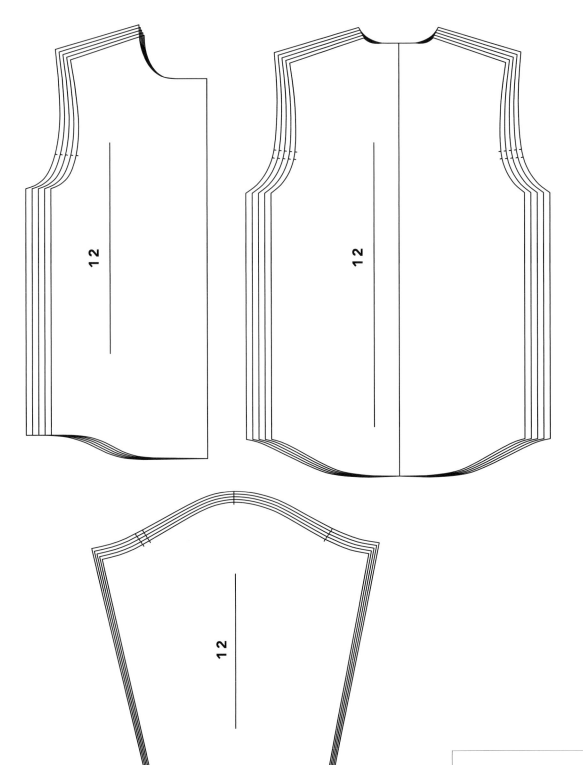

121

FIGURE 121.
A conventionally graded and nested blouse block showing that grading primarily increases size across the body. Holly McQuillan.

Pathway 1:
One-size-fits-most

The need for grading can be eliminated by designing a garment that will fit individuals across a range of sizes. Yeohlee Teng describes such garments as "the ultimate efficiency" (Luther in Major and Teng 2003: 18). Teng's sarong in the "Yield" exhibition (McQuillan and Rissanen 2011: 12–17) is adjustable to almost any waist size. This approach is mainly limited to loose, adjustable, or wrapped garments.

Pathway 2:
Conventional grading

Conventional grading remains an option. The benefit is its familiarity within industry and its speed. The subsequent sizes are likely to create fabric waste; marker planning is not part of conventional grading. Not all components necessarily grade, while the rest may do so unevenly, depending on the garment design. Once each component has been graded, it is unlikely that they will configure within the marker like the original size. Can a claim of zero waste be made of a garment if only the sample size is zero waste?

Pathway 3:
Designing each size

Each size can be redesigned with the original as a guide. Each size is designed to look as much like the sample size as possible, while ensuring that each size is zero waste.

FIGURE 122.
This sarong by Yeohlee Teng (2009) is both zero waste and one size fits all. Like a traditional sarong, the wearer can wrap and tie the garment to fit their body. Yeohlee Teng.

122

This pathway may be time-consuming, but in the context of sustainability, where perhaps we ought to design less and design better, this may become feasible over time. Materialbyproduct in Australia produces size ranges of zero waste garments (Dimasi 2009). Each size is slightly different visually yet in no way compromised; the differences are not accidental.

The designer needs to determine which components need to grade and by how much. These components are given priority in the redesign process, as they set the limits for the pieces that do not necessarily grade (pockets, tabs, etc.) and pieces that grade in one direction only (cuffs, collars, etc.). When it has been determined which components grade, two options emerge for the redesign process: changing or retaining the configuration of the garment components in the marker.

Pathway 3A:
Changing the marker
configuration

Once components have been graded, they are examined on the fabric width to see how they may configure in comparison to the original marker. The marker for Endurance Shirt II (created in 2011) is considerably different from the marker for Endurance Shirt I (created in 2009). Although the two shirts are the same size and thus not directly related to grading, the impact of changing the marker on garment appearance is nonetheless evident. The elbow patches of the first shirt were eliminated in the later one. Our research suggests that retaining the original marker as much as possible would better facilitate retaining design integrity while having each size be zero waste.

Pathway 3B:
Retaining the marker
configuration

A number of possibilities exist for retaining the original marker configuration across sizes.

Relative fullness in a garment

If garments have fullness (fabric considerably larger than the body it covers) designed into the piece, it may be possible to retain the outline of each component to produce a range of sizes. What changes is the relative amount of fullness in a component. Pleats, tucks, darts, and gathers can be employed to control fullness across sizes.

Materialbyproduct has created printed tops and dresses that have a number of vertical pleats through the body. A larger size will have fewer pleats than a smaller one; each size contains the same total amount of fabric (Dimasi 2009). Gathering can be used similarly. The gathered peplum of a blouse by Zandra Rhodes (Rhodes 2005: 32–36) demonstrates this approach. While the waist of the blouse that the peplum joins onto grades in the conventional manner, the peplum component remains the same size across the three sizes. If a larger size range were to be produced, problems could arise, but this method works when three sizes are produced, as in the case of the Rhodes bodice.

The grade amount is usually larger horizontally than vertically, which can make cutting on the lengthwise grain challenging with retaining the marker composition across sizes. Cutting on the cross-wise grain may be a solution in some instances, if the nature of the fabric permits it.

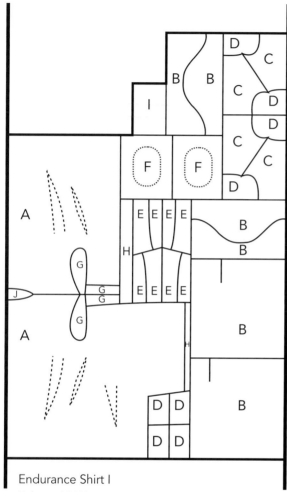

Endurance Shirt I
Fabric: 100% Linen
Fabric width: 135cm
Yield: 176cm

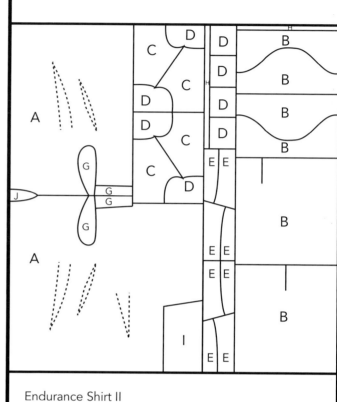

Endurance Shirt II
Fabric: Linen/viscose
Fabric width: 148cm
Yield: 152cm

A: Body
B: Sleeve (including top sleeve lining)
C: Yoke
D: Cuff
E: Collar & stand
F: Elbow patch
G: Sleeve placket
F: Elbow patch
G: Sleeve placket
H: Internal waist stay
I: Internal back pleat stay
J: CB Yoke appliqué

FIGURE 123.
In 2011 Timo Rissanen adopted the
Endurance shirt from 2009 for a new fabric
width, and simplified the design of the shirt
by removing the elbow patches. The two
markers demonstrate that while a zero waste
garment needs to be redesigned for each new
fabric width, the change need not be drastic.
Timo Rissanen.

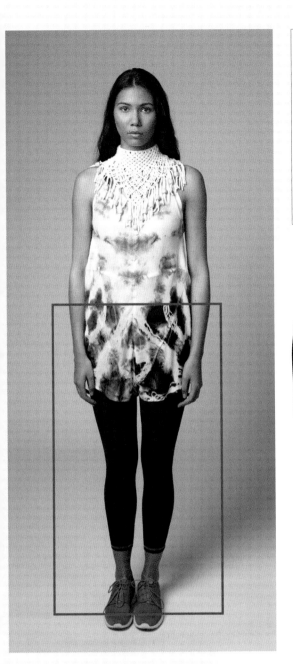

FIGURE 124.
Tights from Gemma Lloyd's 2014
graduate collection: Elutheromania.
Gemma Lloyd.

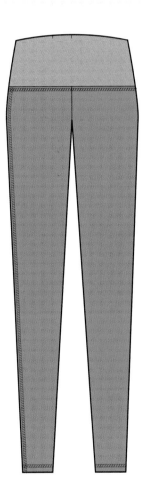

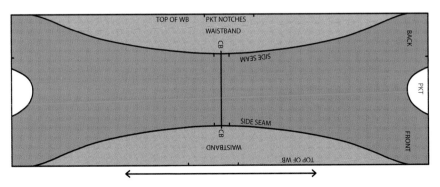

SELVAGE

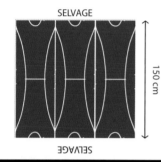

150 cm

SELVAGE

General notes
- 4-way stretch fabric with a width of 150 cm (59¹⁄₁₆ inches).
- one garment fits the entire width of the fabric
- only uses 52.6 cm (20¹¹⁄₁₆ inches) length of fabric.

Sizing considerations
- the width of the hip and thigh area can be widened to accommodate different sizing
- this only alters the curve of the waistband, adding height to the waistband which may be needed with larger sizes

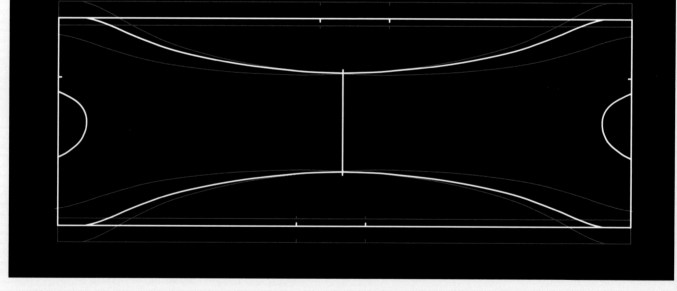

125

FIGURE 125.
Graded pattern from Gemma Lloyd's 2014 graduate collection: Elutheromania. The fabric is a two-way stretch knit, allowing the pattern to be oriented on the cross-wise grain. Gemma Lloyd.

Mixing two sizes in a marker

The marker of the slashed jersey top by Rissanen allows the mixing of two sizes in one marker to facilitate grading. Two garments of the original size (Medium) fit across the fabric width. On the right are a Large and a Small, which also fill the width. There are two limitations with this particular example. The vertical garment length has not graded, although this could be addressed by having a smaller hem allowance on the Large and larger on the Small. The other limitation is that one would be cutting the same number of Smalls and Larges, regardless of the actual orders received.

Pathway 4:
Using a different fabric width for each size

Some historical examples demonstrate an approach that may work for some simple zero waste garments in knitted fabrics. Baumgarten et al. (1999: 60, 108) note how with many historical shirts, the marker did not change when a smaller or larger garment was required. Instead, a narrower or wider fabric was used. In contemporary manufacturing, fabric mills usually impose a minimum quantity per fabric, often in the hundreds of meters; this would likely apply to each width. Knitted fabrics, however, provide an exception. It is not uncommon to see T-shirts and tank tops made from tubular knit fabrics like jersey or rib. These fabrics are knitted in a range of diameters to create a range of sizes. Ensuring each size is zero waste would follow the design of the original size.

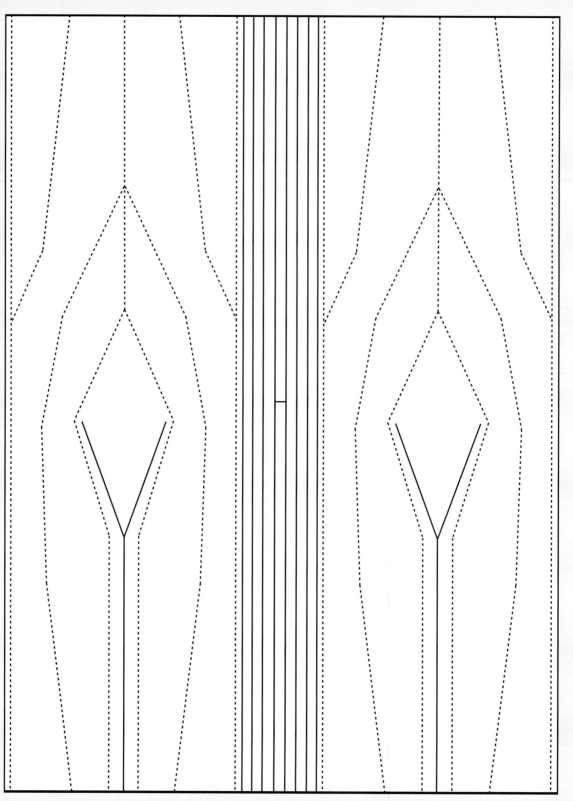

126

FIGURE 126.
Marker for two tank tops in original sample size by
Timo Rissanen (2008); the top was designed to take
up half the width of the fabric. A smaller and larger size
could be placed similarly together, acknowledging that
vertical grading is not accounted for. Timo Rissanen.

Pathway 5:
A hybrid method

Often combinations of the previous four pathways are likely. The top by Rhodes discussed earlier departs from some grading conventions. The outside parameters of the sleeve patterns (see pathway 3B) do not grade, to allow the marker to remain the same across the three sizes. Only the hole that joins the sleeve to the armhole in the bodice, enclosed within the larger square, grades.

To sum, multiple solutions exist in regard to grading, given the variability of garments, the varying size range requirements of a company, and variations in grade rules. The most appropriate solution is determined based on the garment type, garment style, the size range that is required, and fabric type and width. To conclude, grading should become a consideration for, and bridge the gap between, fashion design and manufacturing.

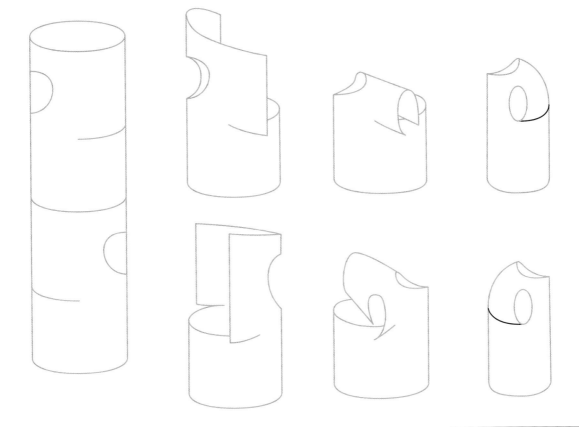

127

FIGURE 127.
David Telfer T-shirt made from circular knit fabric (2010). David Telfer.

FABRIC IN MANUFACTURING ZERO WASTE GARMENTS

A

B

128

C

FIGURE 128.
A variety of selvages utilized as detailing (A), openings (B), and hems (C). The beauty of a fabric's selvage can inform the design process. Photographs by Thomas McQuillan.

Some challenges relating to zero waste fashion design arise from a tension between fashion manufacture and fabric. Since the Industrial Revolution it has been the aim of almost all manufacturing of mass-produced goods to produce uniform, standardized products. The main material of mass-produced clothes, a length of fabric, despite being a mass-produced product in itself, often is not uniform in width, appearance, and other characteristics. Rather than work with the variability of fabric, conventional fashion design and manufacture aim to overcome it.

Extensive strategies to address the variability of fabric exist and some lead to further fabric wastage. Although it would be easy to blame this on manufacturing practices, those practices currently serve fashion design, fashion business, and fashion markets. Rissanen (2013: 114–120) discusses fabric in manufacturing zero waste garments at greater length; the following is an introduction to the issues.

Cutting fabric

A number of issues in fashion manufacture relate to cutting fabric and the impact of fabric's particular properties on cutting practices. Fabric waste as a consideration for fashion design creates specific implications for how some of these issues may be addressed. Perhaps the most significant issue relating to fabric in fashion manufacturing concerns the difference between cutting a single sample garment and cutting multiples during manufacture.

In order to cut multiple garments, the required fabric layers, or plies, are placed on top of each other on the cutting table. A length of fabric is laid down continuously with folds at the end of each ply. Once laid down, the plies constitute a lay. The garments are then cut; for example, if the lay is made of fifty plies and the marker contained one garment, then fifty garments would be cut at once. Tyler states (1991: 69): "Since it is impossible to spread the fabric so that all the plies [layers of fabric in mass production cutting] are aligned precisely, the width of the marker must be made a little narrower than the fabric." This means that only one selvage (fabric edge lengthwise) can be lined up precisely at the cutting stage (Chuter 1995: 129). Tyler (1991: 71) suggests that relatively large variation in fabric width is best addressed by planning "markers to different widths and to sort pieces into batches according to their measured widths; additional labour costs are outweighed by the material savings."

These statements have clear implications for manufacturing zero waste garments, as a zero waste marker is made for a specific width. In practical terms, accommodating variable fabric width might result in variation within the units of a single garment style. We call for a shared inquiry into what might be possible in terms of user acceptance of this variability in garments. Is not allowing such serendipity being truthful to the material, cloth?

Fabric selvages

Selvages are the two long edges of a fabric length. In woven fabrics these are woven in a particular manner to prevent fraying. Some knit fabrics are knitted as a tube and then cut to a flat length, sometimes with glue used on the edges to create stable selvages. Selvages can be wavy, meaning they have not been subject to the same amount of shrinkage as the rest of the fabric. Conversely, selvages can also be tight, meaning they have shrunk more than the fabric. In conventional fashion design and manufacture, selvages are rarely incorporated into the garment design. Cutting them off solves wavy or tight selvages, and it also provides the cutter with a visual confirmation that the plies are aligned. We mostly incorporate selvages into the garments we design, and we encourage you to do the same, selecting fabrics for the beauty of their selvages or conversely for them being almost invisible.

In designing a chambray shirt for Timovsthang, Rissanen incorporated the selvages into the front placket and back yoke (the white stripes in the images below are the selvages), and this shirt was cut in small production runs of multiple garments without any particular difficulty. The fabric was stable and an even width throughout the length, and the small quantities (fifteen or less per size) enabled accurate laying and cutting of the fabric. Similarly, the denim coat by Rissanen uses both selvages as external visual elements. The denim was stable but incorporating both selvages into a zero waste garment in mass-manufacture may require additional problem solving.

Shaeffer (2001: 49–50) discusses the use of selvages to stabilize seams internally in haute couture. The potential of utilizing selvages as structural stabilizing components in ready-to-wear is underexplored; the difference to haute couture is that these would be machine-stitched rather than hand-sewn.

FIGURE 129.
Möbius garment by Yeohlee
(2006) that incorporates selvages.
Yeohlee Teng.

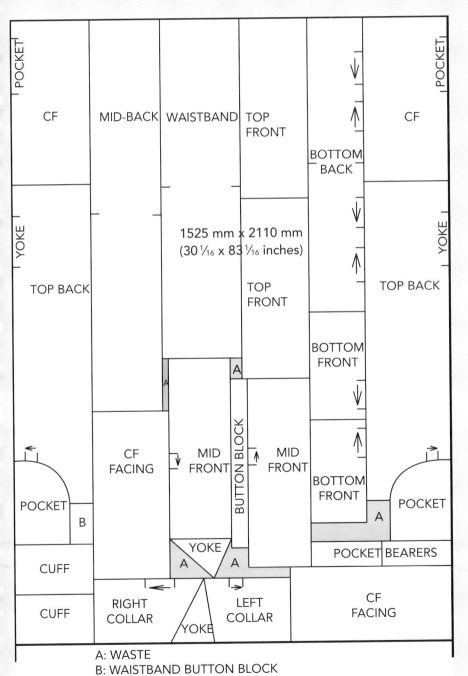

POCKET

CF

MID-BACK | WAISTBAND | TOP FRONT

BOTTOM BACK

CF

POCKET

YOKE

TOP BACK

1525 mm x 2110 mm
(30 1/16 x 83 1/16 inches)

TOP FRONT

YOKE

TOP BACK

BOTTOM FRONT

A

CF FACING | MID FRONT | BUTTON BLOCK | MID FRONT

BOTTOM FRONT

A

POCKET | B

POCKET | BOTTOM FRONT

POCKET

CUFF

YOKE | A | A

POCKET | BEARERS

CUFF | RIGHT COLLAR | LEFT COLLAR | CF FACING

YOKE

A: WASTE
B: WAISTBAND BUTTON BLOCK

130A

FIGURES 130A AND 130B.
Denim coat by Timo Rissanen
(2008) that incorporates both
selvages into the overall aesthetic
of the garment. Figure 130A:
Photograph by Mariano Garcia.
Figure 130B: Timo Rissanen.

130B

Fabric flaws

A fabric flaw is a feature that would diminish the garment, if that part of the fabric was included. The issue of fabric flaws is partly subjective. For example, a hole in a fabric could end up on or near a seam, compromising the structural integrity of the garment; this is safely described as a flaw. On the other hand, a slub or other inconsistency in the weave or knit is usually also considered a flaw, but a visual one. What if such flaws and imperfections were embraced both in design and in use?

This raises questions about our expectations for uniformity in mass-produced garments. What if, for example, a fabric "imperfection" in a garment was embroidered to highlight it? With careful design, this could be possible. It could be that zero-waste fashion design and manufacture, within conventional industry practices and mindsets could magnify some of the challenges that fabric ordinarily poses for garment manufacture. Perhaps we need to be more critical of some conventions, searching for and experimenting with new possibilities.

TARA ST JAMES OF STUDY NY

Tara St James is the founder of Study NY, a design studio with a concern for the environmental and human aspects of the fashion industry. She founded Study NY in 2009, after having worked as the creative director for Covet. She is the winner of the 2011 Ecco Domani Fashion Foundation Award for Sustainable Design.

St James's considered approach to zero waste fashion design and sustained collaborations with artists and textile designers are the key components to her success. She aims to build upon her brand's sustainability and evaluate the chain of production to see where possibilities exist for further transparency. A believer in open sourcing and information sharing, over the years St James has shared her sources and contacts on her blog. By doing so she supports her suppliers, often smaller, fair-trade textile mills and fashion manufacturers.

St James started Study NY with an entirely zero waste collection for spring 2009, and she has continued zero waste fashion design in subsequent seasons. For example, for spring 2011, she created a zero waste skirt from a hand-woven silk ikat from Uzbekistan. Zero waste is one of many aspects of sustainability that she built into the company's core mission.

Several times a year, Study NY (the company no longer subscribes to the traditional fashion calendar, adopting a slower pace of evolution) repeats a version of a square-cut zero waste dress, which can be worn in a number of ways. This is an efficient example of zero waste fashion design, as a square of fabric with intricately placed buttons and buttonholes allows the wearer to play with the garment and find her ideal way of wearing it. This is a deep engagement with waste elimination; fabric and the experience it creates as a garment are equally valued.

FIGURE 131.
Top and trousers by Study NY (2014). A deep respect for fabric is present in all of St James's work; for example, both sides of the fabric are often used. Tara St James.

131

FIGURE 132.
Dress by Study NY (2014) made
of three fabrics. This approach to
design can be used strategically
to use leftover fabric stock while
connecting garments over seasons.
Tara St James.

132

FIGURE 133.
Dress by Study NY (2014), with
a signature open back detail that
has featured on several Study NY
dresses and jackets over the years.
Tara St James.

133

SHORT CUTS

1 Are particular seam types and construction finishes more suitable for zero waste garments than others? Speculate on this using a specific garment type (e.g., tailored jacket).

2 What barriers might exist for designing each size of a garment that results in aesthetic variations from the original sample design?

3 Sketch ten designs that incorporate the fabric selvage either internally, externally, or both.

zero waste fashion design: getting started

In essence this book is unfinished.
The authors do not own zero waste fashion
design; having almost finished reading this
book, you are now invited to write the chapters
that follow. Just as sustainability is not a
destination to get to—it is an ongoing, shared
conversation of questioning and discovery—
there is no "right" place for you to be at to
begin exploring zero waste fashion design.
The authors made many messes and mistakes,
and the learning from those is the foundation
on which this book has grown.

134

FIGURE 134.
Learning from mistakes: Timo Rissanen trying on the second toile of his first attempt at a pair of subtraction cutting trousers during "The Cutting Circle" in 2011. Photograph by Holly McQuillan.

ON INSPIRATION

The word inspiration is chronically misused in fashion. To be inspired is to breathe life into something—inspiration is a formidable force. Yet the superficial referencing prevalent in fashion can hardly be called inspiration. Look up the word in a dictionary, and then ask, when have you been truly inspired?

If you reference the garments of another culture, do so thoughtfully. If you can, engage in conversation with members of that culture; engage deeply. As well as examining what the garments look like, understand their cloth and cut. In 2014 a group of students developed a collection with McQuillan, influenced by traditional dress from Middle Eastern and Asian cultures, with several zero waste garments as references. The students' goal was a unisex, one-size-fits-most collection. The toile stage revealed that the collection could become zero waste relatively easily, due to the reference garments. The students had not practiced zero waste fashion design before, and zero waste was not an initial goal for the project.

Nonetheless they chose zero waste fashion design as the approach for the project. The students used a number of techniques, from geometric pattern shapes to utilizing a modification of a trouser layout discussed in Chapter 3. At times multiple designs were designed together within a single marker to eliminate waste. This project illustrates that, even for beginners, zero waste fashion design can be easy, if the project parameters are kept relatively simple. Only two fabrics (a cotton duck and a single jersey in cotton) and two fabric widths were used for the garments. Looser shapes can provide a safe explorative space for beginners before attempting more complex and fitted zero waste garments.

Even relatively simple shapes provide endless possibilities for variation and exploration. Here basic shapes with multiple possible outcomes are illustrated. These can be explored in half-scale quickly and effectively, before moving to full-scale.

FIGURE 135.
Undivided (2014). A unisex, one-size-fits-most, zero waste fashion collection, designed by second-year Massey University fashion design students, Natalie Procter, Izzy Butle, Shannen Young, Maxwell Wilson, and Shay Minhinnick. Natalie Procter.

FIGURE 136.
It is possible to rapidly generate multiple zero waste
designs from a single simple origin (in this case the T-shirt
pattern shown in Chapters 1 and 3). The patterns shown
here create a range of tops, dresses, and coats, which were
designed by Holly McQuillan in approximately five minutes.
Holly McQuillan.

137A

137B

137C

FIGURE 137A.
Basic T-shirt on narrow, soft, drapey fabric.

FIGURE 137B.
Basic T-shirt on narrow fabric width, structured fabric.

FIGURE 137C.
Basic T-shirt with tapered sleeve and cropped length.

Photographs by Thomas McQuillan.

FIGURE 137D.
Maxi dress in pieced-together fabric.

FIGURE 137E.
Two-tone, color-blocked coat with sculptural sleeve and back.

FIGURE 137F.
Wrap dress.

Photographs by Thomas McQuillan.

137D

137E

137F

INTERVIEW WITH KIA KOSKI

Kia Koski is a Finnish fashion designer and lecturer at Lahti University of Applied Sciences (LUAS) in Finland. In 2010 she was recognized as the Fashion Designer of the Year by Ornamo and Grafia, two national societies for design in Finland, for her accomplishments in Finnish activewear design. Since 2011 Koski has taught a zero waste fashion design course at LUAS.

+ **Back in 2010, how did you think to incorporate zero waste fashion design into teaching at Lahti University of Applied Sciences?**

Back in autumn 2010, we started at the Institute of Design in Lahti University of Applied Sciences (LUAS) a module called Design for Environmental Efficiency. We discussed then what kind of design course could be interesting enough, at our Department of Fashion and Clothing design, and at the same time fulfill the goals mentioned: "The student understands the aim of sustainable and ethical thinking; understands what environmental efficiency in product development means; and, is able to adapt sustainably thinking and practice as a part of the design process."

At that time it was already clear that the students were quite conscious about recycling and sustainability. It was also a trend, and that is why it was easy to incorporate a course that dealt with meaningful and ethical product design.

As a designer and teacher specialized in functional clothing, I was naturally very interested also in the true function and meaning of clothing in general, so I looked for every text and info I could find about sustainable fashion and clothing design. I started my research and background learning before the first course in spring 2011.

The book that was crucial for me was *Sustainable Fashion: Why Now?* (Heathorn and Ulasewicz 2008), followed by *Shaping Sustainable Fashion* (Gwilt and Rissanen 2011). After reading these, with other publications, I was convinced that these were the future trends that we had to incorporate into our design thinking. Janine Benyus, as well as Cradle to Cradle and a few conferences in Denmark and Sweden, opened my eyes to sustainable thinking in the textile and fashion industry. My goal was to find out how to incorporate this thinking into a design praxis that would be challenging and meaningful for the students. Zero waste fashion design was new and interesting. I explored everything I could about it, particularly online, before we started. My aim was to give the students a kickoff that gave them enough challenge and inspiration.

+ Were there any particular challenges with that project, and how did you tackle them?

The biggest challenge was that none of the teachers had experience with zero waste pattern making. I decided from the beginning that I, as a teacher, needed to throw myself into the unknown on the same level as the students. I introduced the goal as an exploration, as a trip into the unknown that we would try to solve together. Both the teacher for pattern making, Marjut Ylä-Mäyry, and I studied and discussed about how to proceed. It was funny that my praxis in pattern making went back to my student years, many, many years ago! So my knowledge about that was almost zero. Luckily we could work together with Marjut when the cutting and sewing started. On the other hand I found it almost as an advantage that I didn't have any specific ideas about pattern making. Julian Roberts was very inspiring in breaking the rules concerning this.

+ Were there any positive surprises about that project?

The most positive surprise was the experimental approach that we had in the first zero waste course and in every course after that. The students really learned by doing. We decided that they would work in pairs, which turned out to be a good decision. When the students work together they explore, make decisions, and encourage each other. The process is more effective.

The first zero waste course was quite simple. The students had 2 meters of white bamboo jersey to work with. They had to design one outfit with one or two pieces. They could dye or print the fabric as they wanted. They also had to arrange a photo shoot and create a poster that we used in an exhibition at the end of the course.

+ How did the students respond to zero waste fashion design?

The response from the students has been very encouraging. They seem to perceive zero waste as something that could be developed as a method, opening new ways of thinking about fashion design methods.

FIGURE 138A.
Dress and vest by Varpu Rapeli
and Ronja Aalto, Lahti University
of Applied Sciences (2011). Kia
Koski; Photograph by Aapo Huhta.

138A

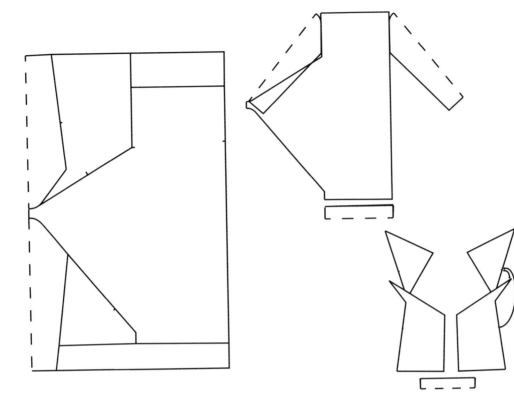

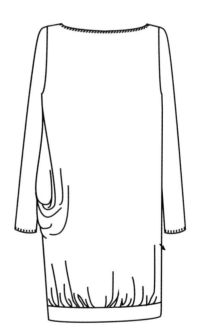

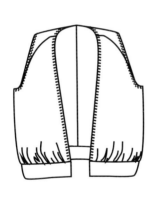

FIGURE 138B.
Dress and vest by Varpu Rapeli
and Ronja Aalto, Lahti University of
Applied Sciences (2011). Kia Koski.

They have learned that you can, so to say, go the other way around and explore what will be the outcome and how to make solutions so that the design meets the goals they set, including the goal of zero material waste. Some students last year already adopted this method in their final theses. One student also thought about how to adapt her zero waste design in an industrial process. The conclusion though was that it's not an easy way to proceed but that there could be possibilities.

+ How has zero waste fashion design "lived on" at LUAS since?

In spring 2015 we are starting our fourth course in zero waste design. Every year we expand on the kind of material to be used. We try to use either roll ends or leftovers from industry, so we sometimes use slightly damaged or otherwise unwanted (though new) materials. Each student pair uses the same amount of the same material.

One important goal along with the design process is to educate the students to be more conscious about the world we live in, and about how the textile and clothing business affects the environment. We do research into new high-tech materials and future trends concerning new developments based on more sustainable solutions in materials and production.

Nature and biomimicry has been a well of inspiration both concerning new materials and construction ideas. I think that explorative research and freedom of making in a context where students experience that they are doing something meaningful is important. At the same time they have to challenge themselves within a quite demanding method of zero waste. This gives them the goal to fulfill their task, and something profound to think about.

139

FIGURE 139.
Design process by Jennifer Backlund
and Anni Tamminen, Lahti University
of Applied Sciences (2014). Kia Koski.

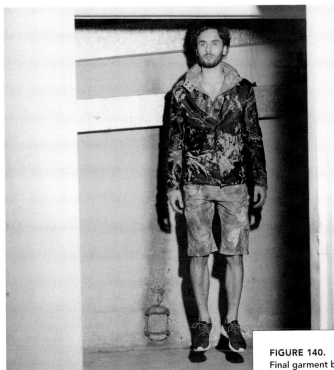

140

FIGURE 140.
Final garment by Jennifer Backlund
and Anni Tamminen, Lahti University
of Applied Sciences (2014). Kia Koski.

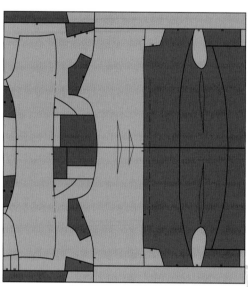

cotton 156 cm x 150 cm (61⅞ x 59⅛ inches), normal marker 215 cm (84⅝ inches)
fabric save = 65 cm (25⅝ inches)

bamboo jersey 152 cm x 222 cm (59¹³⁄₁₆ x 87⅜ inches), normal marker 290 cm (114³⁄₁₆ inches)
fabric save = 68 cm (26¾ inches)

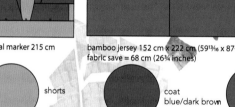

shorts

coat
blue/dark brown

coat gray

141

FIGURE 141.
**Final garment by Jennifer Backlund
and Anni Tamminen, Lahti
University of Applied Sciences
(2014).** Kia Koski.

DOCUMENTING AND
REFLECTING ON DESIGN

It took the authors many messes and mistakes to begin writing a book about zero waste fashion design, as part of an ever-expanding learning process. Mistakes are a natural and necessary part of learning. What has proven crucial is the dual activity of documenting and reflecting on the design process and its results. There is no right way to document. Sketch in a way that works for you. Photograph your patterns as well as your toiles. Write about your process, in a voice that suits you and sounds like you. All of these forms of documentation allow you to then reflect on what you have done, what is working, what is not working, and what the ways forward may be. Reflection allows us to develop mastery, and you ought to document the reflection, too.

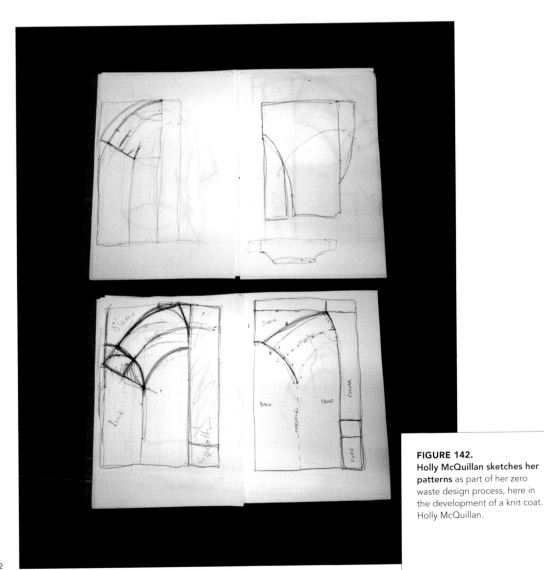

FIGURE 142.
Holly McQuillan sketches her patterns as part of her zero waste design process, here in the development of a knit coat. Holly McQuillan.

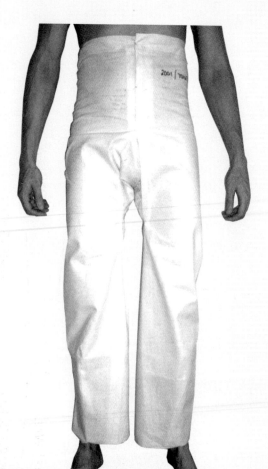

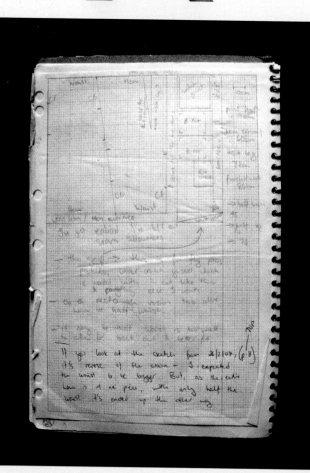

FIGURES 143A AND 143B.
Timo Rissanen designed a square-cut trouser on graph paper (2008), and the first toile was unsatisfactory both in appearance and fit. Critical reflection allowed Rissanen to see the potential in this Thayaht-inspired trouser and to refine it to a successful result in denim. Timo Rissanen.

143A

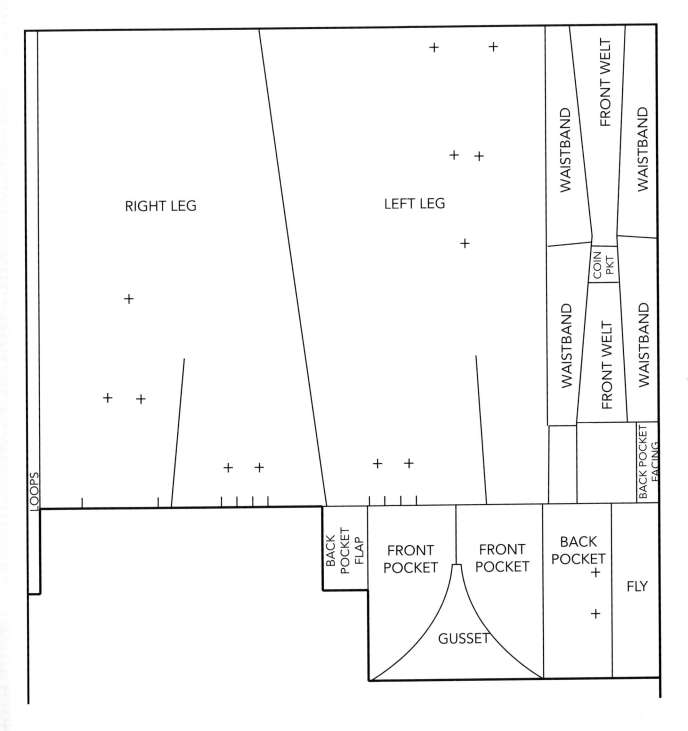

RIGHT LEG

LEFT LEG

LOOPS

WAISTBAND

FRONT WELT

WAISTBAND

WAISTBAND

COIN PKT

FRONT WELT

WAISTBAND

BACK POCKET FACING

BACK POCKET FLAP

FRONT POCKET

FRONT POCKET

BACK POCKET

FLY

GUSSET

ON SHARING

Fashion is traditionally secretive. The authors have shared their ideas, as well as the garments developed alongside patterns, for many years. Contrary to the well-meaning warnings from colleagues and friends, they have not experienced any negative consequences from sharing their work openly. In fact the experience has been overwhelmingly positive. The internet is a global network of "villages" where people with similar interests can come together, share ideas, and learn from one another. Zero waste fashion design is only difficult if you try to do it in isolation; it is a team sport.

FIGURE 144.
"Benefits of collaboration" is a diagram drawn by Julian Roberts during "The Cutting Circle" in 2011. Having this on the studio wall allowed Roberts, McQuillan, and Rissanen to collaborate freely for two weeks. Julian Roberts.

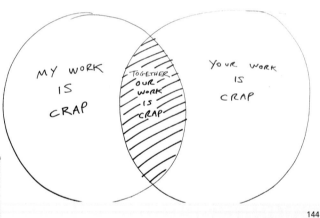

144

FIGURE 145.
"The Cutting Circle" team: Holly McQuillan, Julian Roberts, and Timo Rissanen. Julian Roberts; Holly McQuillan; Timo Rissanen.

145

CONVERSATION WITH YEOHLEE TENG

Yeohlee Teng is an American pioneer of zero waste fashion design, based in New York. Her collections for Yeohlee have included zero waste garments since the early 1980s. In exhibiting her works Teng often includes the patterns alongside the garments, as they provide insights into the thinking processes that led to the garments.

Visit Yeohlee's website here: www.yeohlee.com

The following is an excerpt from a conversation between Rissanen and Yeohlee Teng in October 2014.

+ My first question is about your approach to design: How does pattern making exist within your design process? Looking at your work it seems obvious that pattern making is part of the design process, or at least part of the thinking in some way, part of the logic of your designing. How did that come to be?

I could break it down simply. You know, when people talk about form and function, that really is the foundation, isn't it?

+ Yeah.

And so, my approach does really start with the client. I heard from an old mate, and she told me that we threw a party together when we were kids, and she said that I came in a little skirt that was made out of 36 by 36 inches of fabric. So I think that it was always with me. I don't remember this, but she mentioned that 36 by 36 really resonated with me.

+ That's really interesting she remembers that.

Yes! I wasn't aware of it—but it's a combination of zero waste, frugality, and also, I have a fascination with numbers. So, what resonated with me was not just that I used all the fabric—it's that the fabric is 36 by 36. I'd do anything to see that 36 by 36, I want to see if it had selvage.

+ I was looking at a coat in your store just now, and the center fronts are just the selvage.

Yeah.

+ I don't know what it is about us, because I feel sometimes like I'm a weird designer, but I love the selvage. If it's in any shape or form something that I can incorporate into the garment I will . . .

Yes.

+ Even in garments . . . even when I had my own line, it wasn't zero waste, but a lot of the garments incorporated the selvage, because I love them. But then, most people don't love them.

I don't understand cutting and throwing away the selvage, right? That's to me like the dumbest thing to do. You know, look, you use the selvage you have less sewing. A coat with a selvage—no facing! No interlining! I mean, how fabulous is that?

+ What I love about selvages, they give you the space within which to design.

Right. I wonder how many people think that way. They are your parameters. There's a limit to what you can do, at least across the grain.

+ Cloth itself seems really important to you as a designer. Can you say something about the experience of working with cloth when you're designing?

There are many different responses, because sometimes the fabric engages you immediately. You know, because texture, feel, weight.

+ And it can be a very intuitive thing.

Yeah.

+ It's a very emotional connection to the fabric.

Yes. I probably could go through, like my work, and it would be very obvious, which fabrics resonated. Because then, the work was more . . . intense? Lou Kahn said that a brick tells you what it wants to do. And fabric, they're all bricks.

FIGURE 146.
Coat by Yeohlee (1997).
Yeohlee Teng.

146

+ That reminds me, a student asked me once, like, what inspires me? And I said, for me it always comes back to that relationship between the body and the cloth and how they interact, and that is a never-ending source of fascination. Like I know that it will fascinate me to the day I die.

+ The way I see zero waste, it's really, it's the celebration of cloth. It is that fascination with numbers as well. Even for people who think that they're not good with numbers.

Can I show you something?

+ Please do.

[Yeohlee shows three dresses in her book.]

It was the most expensive fabric I had encountered. I really loved it, and I wanted to work with it, and I figured out mathematically that I could afford 7 meters, which is 7.7 yards. So, I was determined to get three gowns out of it. In that process, an accident happened, a design detail happened as a direct result. Of the ends of the fabric, and it's this. [She points to piece at waist of one gown.] It's my most treasured moment of zero waste, you see, that detail.

+ I actually wrote about this in my PhD.

You did?

+ I did, because I had speculated that sometimes it might be more feasible to design multiple zero waste garments together. Holly McQuillan has designed multiple garments together as well.

We had a moment recently: this cotton was maybe 42 inches wide, and the piece was 51 yards, and the garment was crescented in the back, on the bias. There were four crescents, and they each had the grain lines going this way. The marker that came had a lot of waste. So, we took it upon ourselves to redo the marker, and we got exactly what we wanted out of it, and my cutter, at the end of the day, brought me 6 inches of the fabric and said, "This is what I have left."

+ That's amazing.

We used up everything. If we went by the yardage, we wouldn't have gotten the yield that we needed.

+ It's remarkable that you actually are able to tell that story, because most fashion designers don't have any stories about markers. They've never even seen one. There is this . . .

Disconnect.

+ Disconnect between design and manufacturing. It's so beautiful to hear of a designer who is involved, because marker making is a problem-solving process.

Yes. It was a beautiful moment. It took the whole team to do it. You know, designers stand on the shoulders of many other people. Those are the people that need the recognition. I feel very passionately about that.

147

FIGURE 147.
Three gowns by Yeohlee (1992), designed and cut together to maximize fabric usage. Yeohlee Teng.

FUTURES FOR ZERO WASTE FASHION DESIGN

Two projects point out that zero waste fashion design is not "good" in and of itself; it needs to be examined in a broader context. Entirely new ways of thinking about how the fashion industry could exist and function (see Tham 2015), while allowing humanity to flourish, are required (see Ehrenfeld 2015). This points toward a new, expanded vision for fashion design: as well as designing and making garments, fashion design ought to participate in the design of the wearing and using of garments, and it ought to design, collaboratively with other fields, the systems in which the wearing and using occurs. These two projects by the authors are among a growing number hinting at such futures in the present.

FIGURE 148.
MakeUse cropped T-shirt (2013) explores user modifiable zero waste garment design. Holly McQuillan.

MakeUse by Holly McQuillan, ongoing since 2012

To date the relationship between zero waste fashion design and the user experience has been underexplored. Dr. Kate Fletcher (2011) has led the Local Wisdom project since 2009. Starting in 2012, McQuillan (2014) has worked on an offshoot of the project, titled MakeUse, to investigate connections between zero waste fashion design and the fashion user experience. Her goal is to develop garments that invite the user to interact deeply with his/her wardrobe, with the related goal of slowing fashion consumption. By enriching the user/product relationship, MakeUse proposes ongoing and evolving use for all garments. The construction in each MakeUse garment is simplified, and the potential use life is extended through the enabling of ongoing modifications and the application of "conspicuous mending." MakeUse acknowledges the different skill and enthusiasm levels that all users bring to any activity and caters to a variety of makers and users by offering the product in varying stages of completion and intervention.

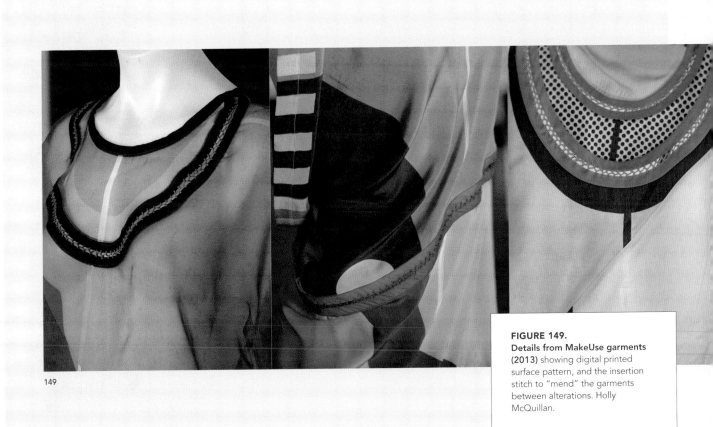

149

FIGURE 149.
Details from MakeUse garments (2013) showing digital printed surface pattern, and the insertion stitch to "mend" the garments between alterations. Holly McQuillan.

The MakeUse garments have been designed for a 120-centimeter-wide cloth; by rotating the grain line, the length or width of the garment can be modified for a different width. A direct relationship between two-dimensional pattern and cloth, and three-dimensional garment is articulated in order for makers/users to better understand the possible forms and modifications available to them. Digital printing and digital embroidery are used to provide guides and hints for the user/maker within the cloth.

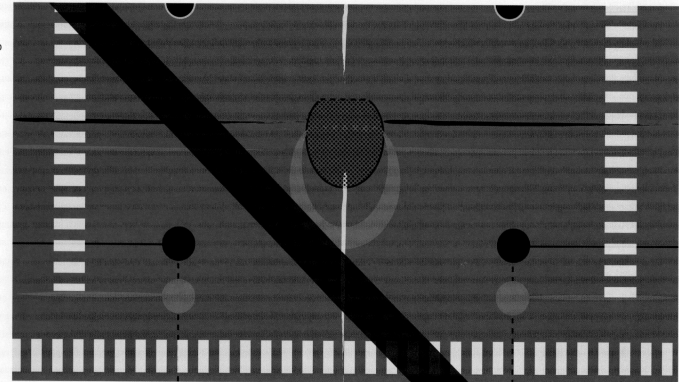

150

FIGURE 150.
MakeUse cropped T-shirt pattern (2013). This digitally printed pattern embeds aspects of the construction process in the aesthetic of the print. Holly McQuillan.

FIGURE 151.
MakeUse cropped T-shirt (2013).
Holly McQuillan.

152

FIGURE 152.
MakeUse uses digital print to assist with the construction and ongoing modification of the garments. The print is both aesthetic and instructional. Holly McQuillan.

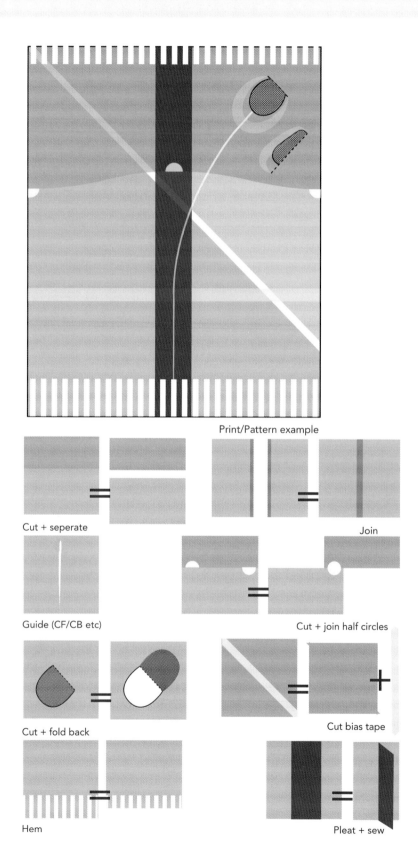

Print/Pattern example

Cut + seperate

Join

Guide (CF/CB etc)

Cut + join half circles

Cut + fold back

Cut bias tape

Hem

Pleat + sew

Degree of involvement

Cost

fully-finished garment

fully sewn garment - necklines/armholes uncut

digitally printed and embroidered cloth

digitally printed cloth

digital print/embroidery file

basic pattern without print information

153

The goals for the final kimono, cropped T-shirt, dress, and trousers were to have a pared-down silhouette, be simple to sew, and have the ability to be modified easily over time. Each pattern had multiple modifications embedded. For example, the dress has two body types, two sleeve types, two armhole shapes and sizes, and two neckline depths. It can be altered for different sizes and lengths easily. The digital print guides the user in these modifications while contributing to the visual aesthetic of the garment.

A visual mapping system was designed to aid in making the garment and in modifying it later. Instructions, such as where to cut, fold, and join, are printed directly onto the garment. The four patterns generated through this process are available for download on the project website (www.makeuse.info).

MakeUse garments are proposed to be part of a larger system designed to encourage the ongoing and iterative use of the products. Existing within a cradle-to-cradle system, MakeUse disrupts the dominant fashion consumption flow from producer to consumer to waste. Product possibilities are proposed by the designer, as deliberately open for modification by the user. Multiple avenues of access and cost exist, depending on the user's choices. This model of engagement encourages the re-localization of manufacturing and aims to foster engagement with local businesses and communities. The garments can be digitally printed and embroidered at local facilities in a distributed manufacturing model. Finishing occurs locally, either by the user or by a seamstress. During the use phase, iterative use and modification are supported by an online community of makers and users, digital instructional information, and by the garments themselves. Once the physical or aesthetic demands of the user cannot be met by the garment, the single fiber garment can be reclaimed, composted, or recycled, depending on the fiber type and the condition of the material.

While many products employing mass customization have been developed, to date very few have been developed through zero waste fashion design or sought to transform the fashion consumer into a fashion user—an active agent in the ongoing use of clothing. MakeUse challenges the dominant "monological" (Fletcher 2014) discourse on fashion as consumption.

Endurance shirts by Timo Rissanen, ongoing since 2009

On a smaller scale, with focus specifically on repair and alteration, Rissanen (2011) has explored designing for repair in the Endurance shirt series from 2009 onward, followed by a cardigan series begun in 2012. Using the fabric's selvages as external seam finishes aims to communicate the zero waste nature of the shirt to the user; the selvage is a reminder of the cloth. The aim for these garments is to connect the designer-maker and user through easy craft techniques (hand running stitch) over time. The designer-maker initiates these when the garment is first made, and as in McQuillan's MakeUse project, the user continues these when the need arises.

Each Endurance shirt is designed and made with future alteration and repair as considerations. The objective of the hand quilting at the back waist and in the elbow patches is to suggest explicit mending, so that later visible repair or alteration, regardless of the user's skill level, would not compromise the garments aesthetically. Furthermore, "surplus" fabric is designed into the garments to facilitate these activities. An internal patch at the back waist in the main fabric could be replaced with another fabric if the patch were required elsewhere in the garment. Equally, the elbow patches have excess fabric folded underneath should it be required later.

The first Endurance shirt made in 2009 ripped in 2012 and a patch was quilted on with a contrast thread, to visually facilitate later repairs even further. There is no end point to the project, as time only enriches it. Shirts and cardigans will be altered and mended, they may be passed from one user to another, and new users will enter the project.

FIGURE 154.
Variations of the Endurance shirt by Rissanen (2008–2014) exploring ideas of repair and alteration with different fabrics, from Irish linen to a 1960s Marimekko curtain. Starting in 2015 the project expands to redesigning the shirt for specific users, adopting the design to their body shape and size, and personal taste and lifestyle needs. Timo Rissanen.

154

FIGURE 155A.
Cardigan by Rissanen (2012)
designed with tartan woven by
Lochcarron of Scotland for Pamela
Vanderlinde, based on a print by
Sonia Delaunay. Not constrained
by commercial necessity to
produce multiples, Rissanen tends
to work with fabrics with stories.
Photograph by Mariano Garcia.

155A

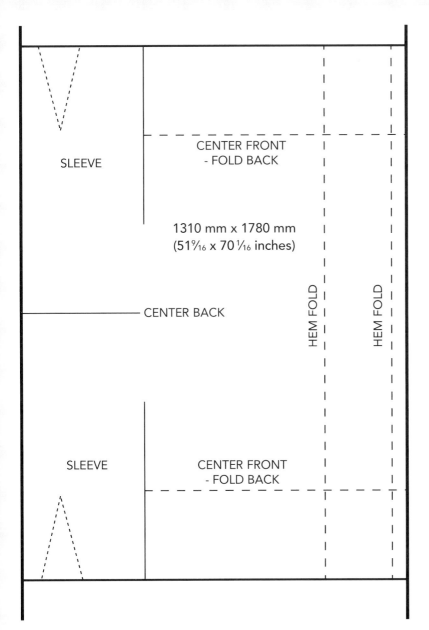

SLEEVE

CENTER FRONT - FOLD BACK

1310 mm x 1780 mm
(51⁹⁄₁₆ x 70¹⁄₁₆ inches)

CENTER BACK

HEM FOLD

HEM FOLD

SLEEVE

CENTER FRONT - FOLD BACK

FIGURE 155B.
The cut of the cardigan is based on the Danish blouse in Figure 4. Elbow darts shape the sleeves and a gusset is inserted into a slash at the back neck, accommodating the top of the back while creating a small shawl collar. Pockets are built into the deep hem. Timo Rissanen.

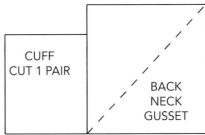

CUFF
CUT 1 PAIR

BACK
NECK
GUSSET

155B

The projects by McQuillan and Rissanen were guided by the following call to designerly arms by Tonkinwise (2005): "Design timely things, things that can last longer by being able to change over time. Design things that are not finished, things that can keep on by keeping on being repaired and altered, things in motion." Ehrenfeld (2015) has called sustainability "the possibility that humans and other life will flourish on the planet forever." We do not yet know all there is to know about that possibility. We can, however, distinguish countless actions that we are all capable of in order to make that possibility a reality now. Zero waste fashion design is a set of actions well worth taking in that respect, and we invite you to join us in that.

FIGURE 156.
Zero waste leggings by Timo Rissanen (2008) use applique as a visual tool to create a deliberate confusion of line overall while also highlighting the body in particular areas. Photograph by Mariano Garcia.

SHORT CUTS

1 List ten mistakes you have made while designing and making garments, and list what you learned from each one.

2 Using MakeUse as a case study, consider why the context in which zero waste fashion design occurs is important.

3 What kind of a future do you want to create for fashion and for yourself in it?

Glossary

Biomimicry

The design and production of materials, structures, and systems that are modeled on biological entities and processes.

Block

A basic pattern developed on paper by drafting or in cloth by draping, with seam allowances omitted (womenswear patterns in New Zealand) or included (UK, Australia, USA), used as a tool to create other patterns. See Sloper.

Computer-Aided Design (CAD)

The use of computer software to aid in the design and production of garments. Examples used in fashion include Adobe Creative Suite (Photoshop, Illustrator, etc.), Gerber, Lectra, Optitex.

Creative Pattern Cutting

Pattern cutting/making that extends beyond basic/reactive approaches, instead exploring pattern making as a creative, generative design process. See Transformation Reconstruction, Subtraction Cutting.

Cut and Drape

A zero waste design strategy begun by cutting part of a garment design into the cloth and then primarily developed on the dress form responding directly to the cloth.

Digital Embroidery

An embroidery process whereby an embroidery machine guided by a computer is used to create patterns on textiles. See Computer-Aided Design.

Digital Textile Print

Any ink-jet-based method of printing colorants onto fabric. See Computer-Aided Design.

Drape

Design and pattern cutting done primarily in three dimensions on the dress form/mannequin. The draped fabric pattern is usually translated into a two-dimensional pattern.

Embodied Energy/Resource

The energy/resources consumed by all of the processes associated with the production of a garment, from the production and processing of natural and manmade resources to manufacturing, transport, and delivery of final product.

Fiber Extraction

The process by which fibers are extracted from raw materials (chemical or organic).

Fixed Areas/Details

A zero waste design strategy where areas or details of a garment are predetermined in shape and/or placement.

Flat Pattern Cutting

Pattern cutting that is developed exclusively in the two-dimensional form. See Drape.

Flexible Areas/Details

A zero waste design strategy where areas or details of a garment are open ended in shape and placement.

Futurism

An artistic movement begun in Italy in 1909 that strongly rejected traditional forms and embraced the energy and dynamism of modern technology, or concern with events and trends of the future, or that anticipate the future.

Geo Cut

A zero waste design strategy that utilizes simple geometric forms to generate garment designs.

Grading

A process that takes a base size to generate all other sizes of the same design, while attempting to maintain design features and proportion.

Haute Couture

Fashion that is constructed by hand from start to finish; made from high quality, expensive, often unusual fabric; sewn with extreme attention to detail; and finished by the most experienced and capable sewers. In France an industry body governs the use of the term "haute couture."

Hierarchy (fashion)

The system in which participants of the fashion industry are ranked (and often separated) according to relative status or authority. The conventional fashion hierarchy usually places the designer at its apex.

Laser Cutting
Digital fabrication process utilizing a laser to cut through fabric, enabling precise cutting and in polyester fabrics welded edges that will not easily fray.

Lay
Multiple layers of cloth (plies).

Layout
Arrangement of pattern pieces in the marker.

Made to Measure
A garment made to fit a specific person.

Marker
A cutting guide showing the most efficient placement of the pattern pieces on the width of cloth. Industry average yield is 85 percent, resulting in 15 percent unused cloth.

Mass Customization
A marketing and manufacturing technique that combines the flexibility and personalization of "custom-made" with the low unit costs associated with mass production.

Mass Production
The production of large amounts of standardized products, including and especially on assembly lines. This is the dominant manufacturing model in the fashion industry.

Minimal Seaming
A fashion design process leading to a reduction in seams needed to produce a garment, which, in turn, ideally leads to greater efficiencies in cutting and sewing.

Modular
Designed with standardized units that can be fit together in a variety of ways.

Negative Space
The space between key garment pattern pieces. In zero waste design (as in art), the negative space is equally important as the pattern shapes that define it.

Nesting (grading)
Where all sizes of a graded pattern are nested inside each other.

Offshore (manufacturing)
Production of garments in a different country to their design.

One-Size-Fits-Most/All
Where garments are designed to fit a range of sizes, through fastenings that allow for alteration of fit (drawstrings or ties for example) or through an oversized aesthetic.

Open Design
An object/product designed to be open to modification and redesign, often shared freely.

Pattern
The two-dimensional template from which the parts of a garment are traced onto fabric before being cut out and assembled.

It determines the three-dimensional form alongside fabric, color, and finishing processes.

Pattern Cutter/Maker
Someone who makes patterns. In smaller or high-end companies, the pattern cutter/maker may work with a designer; in larger companies it may be a distinctly separate role from design with limited interaction.
See Hierarchy.

Pattern Cutting/Making
Process by which a drawn design is translated into a two-dimensional pattern that creates the final garment.

Planned Chaos
A zero waste fashion design technique utilizing garment blocks to plan the layout.

Ply
A single layer of fabric.

Postconsumer Textile Waste
Textile waste (garments and household textiles) created by consumers when they are no longer needed, wanted, or functional.

Preconsumer Textile Waste
Textile waste created by producers, generated at a variety of stages through the production process, including fiber processing, fabric manufacturing, and garment production. The majority of preconsumer textile waste is generated in garment production.

Re-localization

Relocating aspects of garment manufacture in the country of consumption.

Ready-to-Wear

Garments designed for large-scale manufacture to a size range, not made to measure.

Sample

Prototype of garment design created in final fabric, which is used to test design and fit, as well as for quality control.

Scale (half/full)

Full-scale, full-size pattern. Half-scale pattern at 50 percent.

Seam

A line where two pieces of fabric are sewn together in a garment. There are a variety of seam types, depending on desired function, fabric type, and aesthetic required.

Seam Allowance

Additional fabric at the perimeter of the pattern to allow for sewing, without compromising fit, and to ensure sufficient durability in use.

Selvage

A self-finished edge of fabric. The selvages keep the fabric from unraveling or fraying. The selvages are a result of how the fabric is created.

Sloper

Primarily a US term for a basic pattern developed on paper by drafting or in cloth by draping, with seam allowances omitted, used as a tool to create other patterns. See Block.

Standardized

The process of developing and implementing technical standards. Standardization in fashion is usually to help maximize repeatability and/or quality of a design.

Subtraction Cutting

A pattern design and cutting process invented by Julian Roberts where the garment form is generated through the removal of cloth from the fabric, creating space for the body to travel through.

Sustainability

Often defined as "meeting the needs of the present without compromising the ability of future generations to meet their needs." This definition is problematic as the nature and scope of needs is subject to interpretation.

Tailors Matrix

The conventional grid of horizontal and vertical guidelines used by tailors to develop garments for the body.

Tessellation

Geometric shapes able to be repeated so there are no gaps between each piece.

The Plug

Developed by Julian Roberts, this technique is based on the premise that any shape can be sewn into any void, so long as the perimeters (minus seam allowance) are the same.

Toile

An initial prototype of a garment design, usually made in an inexpensive cloth such as calico/muslin.

Transformation Reconstruction

A pattern cutting technique developed by Shingo Sato that combines dart manipulation/ elimination and form creation with drawing directly on the toile.

Upcycling

Using a low-value material to generate a higher-value product.

Use Practices

The actions that users of products undertake.

Zero Waste

Lifestyles and practices that emulate sustainable natural cycles, where any/all discarded materials are designed to become resources for others to use.

Zero Waste Fashion

The design and manufacture of fashion that aims to eliminate the production of textile waste. See Postconsumer Textile Waste and Preconsumer Textile Waste.

References

Aakko, M., and K. Niinimäki (2014), "Experimenting with Zero-Waste Fashion Design," in K. Niinimäki (ed.), *Sustainable Fashion: New Approaches*, 68–79, Helsinki: Aalto University.

Aldrich, W. (2013), *Fabrics and Pattern Cutting*, Chichester: John Wiley and Sons Ltd.

Almond, K. (2010), "Insufficient Allure: The Luxurious Art and Cost of Creative Pattern Cutting," *International Journal of Fashion Design, Technology and Education*, 3 (1): 15–24.

Baumgarten, L., J. Watson, and F. Carr (1999), *Costume Close-up. Clothing Construction and Pattern 1750–1790*, Williamsburg, VA, and New York: The Colonial Williamsburg Foundation in association with Quite Specific Media Group, Ltd.

Burnham, D. K. (1973), *Cut My Cote*, Toronto: Royal Ontario Museum.

Campbell, M. (2010), "The Development of a Hybrid System for Designing and Pattern Making In-set Sleeves," PhD thesis, RMIT, Melbourne.

Climer, G. (2013), "The Cranial Cut: Creating a Pattern for the Human Face," *International Journal of Fashion Design, Technology and Education*, 6 (2): 99–103.

Cooklin, G. (1997), *Garment Technology for Fashion Designers*, Oxford: Blackwell Science.

de Marly, D. (1980), *The History of Haute Couture 1850–1950*, London: B. T. Batsford.

Dimasi, S. (2009), "Materialbyproduct," *Fashioning Now Symposium*, University of Technology Sydney, July 28, 2009. Available online: http://fashioningnow.com (accessed January 10, 2010).

Ehrenfeld, J. R. (2015), "The Real Challenge of Sustainability," in K. Fletcher and M. Tham, *Routledge Handbook of Sustainability and Fashion*, London: Routledge.

Fasanella, K. (1998), *The Entrepreneur's Guide to Sewn Product Manufacturing*, Las Cruces, NM: Kathleen Fasanella.

Fasanella, K. (2006), "What Is a Block?" *Fashion Incubator*, blog. Available online: http://www.fashion-incubator.com/archive/what_is_a_block (accessed July 16, 2014).

Fasanella, K. (2010), "Pattern Puzzle: Shingo Sato," *Fashion Incubator*, blog. Available online: http://www.fashion-incubator.com/archive/pattern-puzzle-shingo-sato (accessed May 12, 2014).

Fletcher, K. (2011), "Post-growth Fashion and the Craft of Users," in A. Gwilt and T. Rissanen (eds.), *Shaping Sustainable Fashion. Changing the Way We Make and Use Clothes*, London: Earthscan.

Fletcher, K. (2014), *Sustainable Fashion and Textiles. Design Journeys*, second edition, London: Routledge.

Fletcher, K., and L. Grose (2012), *Fashion and Sustainability. Design for Change*. London: Laurence King Publishing.

Fry, T. (2009), *Design Futuring. Sustainability, Ethics and New Practice*. Sydney: University of New South Wales Press.

Gugnani, A., and A. Mishra (2012), *Textile & Apparel Compendium 2012*, Technopak.

Hishinuma, Y. (ed.) (1986), *Clothes by Yoshiki Hishinuma*, Tokyo: Yobisha, Co.

Kirke, B. (1998), *Madeleine Vionnet*, San Francisco: Chronicle Books.

Lindqvist, R. (2013), "On the Logic of Pattern Cutting: Foundational Cuts and Approximations of the Body," Licenciate thesis, University of Borås Studies in Artistic Research, Borås.

Major, J. S., and Y. Teng (eds.) (2003), *Yeohlee: Work. Material Architecture*, Mulgrave: Peleus Press.

McDonough, W., and M. Braungart (2002), *Cradle to Cradle. Remaking the Way We Make Things*, New York: North Point Press.

McQuillan, H. (2011), "Zero-Waste Design Practice. Strategies and Risk Taking for Garment Design," in A. Gwilt and T. Rissanen (eds.), *Shaping Sustainable Fashion. Changing the Way We Make and Use Clothes*, 83–97, London: Earthscan.

McQuillan, H., and T. Rissanen (2011), *Yield: Making Fashion without Waste* [Exhibition catalog], New York.

McQuillan, H., T. Rissanen, and J. Roberts (2013), "The Cutting Circle: How Making Challenges Design," *Research Journal of Textiles and Apparel*, 17 (1): 39–49.

Nakamichi, T. (2010), *Pattern Magic*, London: Laurence King Publishing.

Niinimäki, K. (2013), "A Renaissance in Material Appreciation: Case Study in Zero Waste Fashion," *Journal of Textile Design Research and Practice*, 1 (1): 77–92.

Rennolds Milbank, C. (1985), *Couture. The Great Designers*, New York: Stewart, Tabori & Chang.

Rissanen, T. (2007), "Types of Fashion Design and Patternmaking Practice," *Nordes 2007*. Available online: http://www.nordes.org/opj/index.php/n13/article/view/185 (accessed March 26, 2015).

Rissanen, T. (2011), "Designing Endurance," in A. Gwilt and T. Rissanen (eds.), *Shaping Sustainable Fashion. Changing the Way We Make and Use Clothes*, 127–138, London: Earthscan.

Rissanen, T. (2013), "Zero-Waste Fashion Design: A Study at the Intersection of Cloth, Fashion Design and Pattern Cutting," PhD thesis, University of Technology Sydney, Sydney.

Rissanen, T. (2015), "The Fashion System through a Lens of Zero-Waste Fashion Design," in K. Fletcher & M. Tham, *Routledge Handbook of Sustainability and Fashion*, London: Routledge.

Rudofsky, B. (1947), *Are Clothes Modern?* Chicago: Paul Theobald.

Rudofsky, B. (1977), *Architecture without Architects: A Short Introduction to Non-pedigreed Architecture*, London: Academy Editions.

Sevin-Doering, G. (2007), *Itineraire—Du costume de theater à la coupe en un seul morceau*. Les editions du jongleur, Colombes.

Shaeffer, C. B. (2001), *Couture Sewing Techniques*, Newtown, CT: The Taunton Press.

Tham, M. (2015), "Futures of Futures Studies in Fashion," in K. Fletcher & M. Tham, *Routledge Handbook of Sustainability and Fashion*, London: Routledge.

Tilke, M. (1956), *Costume Patterns and Designs: A Survey of Costume Patterns and Designs of All Periods and Nations from Antiquity to Modern Times*, London: A. Zwemmer Ltd.

Tonkinwise, C. (2005), "Is Design Finished? Dematerialisation and Changing Things," in A-M. Willis (ed.), *Design Philosophy Papers*, collection two, 20–30, Ravensbourne: Team D/E/S.

Zandra Rhodes: A Lifelong Love Affair with Textiles [Exhibition catalog] (2005), Woodbridge, England: Antique Collectors' Club.

Index

Numbers followed by f indicate a figure caption.

Acknowledgments

We sincerely thank our commissioning editor, Colette Meacher, and textbook development editor, Miriam Davey, at Bloomsbury for your support and patience in bringing this book into existence. Thank you to everyone at Lachina and to Evelin Kasikov for the dedication throughout the production of this book.

We have both been generously funded at our respective universities over the years, and we thank Massey University College of Creative Arts and School of Fashion at Parsons School of Design for funding that supported the creation and documentation of many of the examples of our work included in this book.

At Massey University, we thank Deb Cumming, Jennifer Whitty, Jen Archer-Martin, Emma Fox Dewin, Karl Kane, Jo Bailey, Nina Weaver, Mary-Ellen Imlach, Tina Downes, and Sue Prescott.

At Parsons School of Design, we thank Joel Towers, Simon Collins, Yvonne Watson, Hazel Clark, Shelley Fox, Fiona Dieffenbacher, Greg Climer, Jonathan KYLE Farmer, Anke Gruendel, Marie Genevieve Cyr, Josephine Tirado, Susana Aguirre, and Jessica Shroyer.

A project like this would not be possible without our many supporters and contributors, and we would like to thank the following individuals: Kate Fletcher, Lynda Grose, Yeohlee Teng, Zandra Rhodes, Winifred Aldrich, Val Horridge, Julia Raath, Cameron Tonkinwise, Sally McLaughlin, Zoe Sadokierski, Julian Roberts, Rickard Lindqvist, Shingo Sato, Alexandra Palmer, Owyn Ruck, Sass Brown, Kia Koski, Minna Cheung, Amy DuFault, Sandra Ericson, Tara St James, Kevin Almond, Maja Stabel, Julia Lumsden, Lela Jacobs, Radu Stern, Mariano Garcia, Yitzhak Abecassis, Simone Austen, Laura Poole, David Valencia, Kirsi Niinimäki, Maarit Aakko, Anita McAdam, Kate Goldsworthy, Rebecca Earley, David Telfer, Kathleen Fasanella, Genevieve Packer, Gemma Lloyd, Natalie Procter, Izzy Butle, Shannen Young, Maxwell Wilson, Shay Minhinnick, Varpu Rapeli, Ronja Aalto, Jennifer Backlund, Anni Tamminen, Carla Fernandez, Samuel Formo, Caroline Priebe, Natalie Chanin, Farid Chenoune, Arti Sandhu, Marie O'Mahony, Karen Giard, Adrienne Perlstein, John Quinn, Juha Arvid Helminen, Noora Pajari, and Emma Haikonen.

The following institutions have been generous in their advice and support over the years, and we thank you: The Dowse Art Museum, Textile Arts Center, Royal Ontario Museum, The Colonial Williamsburg Foundation, San Diego History Society, John Wiley and Sons Ltd, Condé Nast, Hearst Corporation, and Lahti University of Applied Sciences.

We thank all of our past and present students for all that we have learned from you.

Finally, we thank our partners and families who make it possible for us to do the work that we do: Thomas, Theodore, and Magnus McQuillan; George Plionis. Thank you.

Credits

Image on page 6 Long Coat and Wrap Skirt from Holly McQuillan's Make/Use V2 project (2015). Photography by Bonny Stewart-MacDonald.

Figure 1 Nothing nothing dress/Julian Roberts

Figure 2 Pattern for Man's Coat. Japanese, Early 20th century; Dorothy K. Burnham/Royal Ontario Museum

Figure 3 Chinese trousers in Tilke (1956)/Ernst Wasmuth Verlag

Figure 4 Blouse from Denmark, in Tilke (1956)/Ernst Wasmuth Verlag

Figure 5 Blouse from Finland (circa 1923)/Timo Rissanen

Figure 6 Coat by Teng (1997)/Yeohlee Teng

Figure 7 Cardigan by Rissanen (2014)/Timo Rissanen

Figure 8 Pattern for Man's Shirt. South American, Possibly Chile; Dorothy K. Burnham/Royal Ontario Museum

Figure 9A Square-cut shirt (1775–1790, featured in Baumgarten et al, 1999)/The Colonial Williamsburg Foundation. Bequest of Grace Hartshorn Westerfield.

Figure 9B Square-cut shirt (1775–1790, featured in Baumgarten et al, 1999) Pattern/The Colonial Williamsburg Foundation. Bequest of Grace Hartshorn Westerfield.

Figure 10 The cut of Thayaht tuta (1919)/Private collection. All rights reserved.

Figure 11 Women's tuta dress/Courtesy of Radu Stern, from *Against Fashion: Clothing as Art, 1850–1930*, by Radu Stern, published by The MIT Press

Figure 12 Aldrich on circular cutting/Winifred Aldrich and John Wiley and Sons Limited

Figure 13A Dress by Zandra Rhodes/San Diego History Center

Figure 13B Pattern by Zandra Rhodes/Zandra Rhodes

Figure 14 (all photos) Sarong by Yeohlee Teng (2009)/Yeohlee Teng

Figure 15 Dress, trousers and top by Holly McQuillan, digital print by Genevieve Packer (2011)/Holly McQuillan; Photograph by Thomas McQuillan

Figure 16 Coat and leggings by Timo Rissanen (2008)/Timo Rissanen; Photograph by Thomas McQuillan

Figure 17 Dress by Study NY by Tara St James (2010)/Tara St James; Photograph by Thomas McQuillan

Figure 18 Dress by Caroline Priebe (2009)/Caroline Priebe; Photograph by Thomas McQuillan

Figure 19 Jacket by Samuel Formo (2010)/Samuel Formo; Photograph by Thomas McQuillan

Figure 20 Three-piece suit by Jennifer Whitty (2011)/Jennifer Whitty; Photograph by Thomas McQuillan

Figure 21 Shirt and Jacket by Julia Lumsden (2010)/Julia Lumsden; Photograph by Thomas McQuillan

Figure 22 Dress by Carla Fernandez (2008)/Carla Fernandez; Photograph by Thomas McQuillan

Figure 23 Coat by David Telfer (2010)/David Telfer; Photograph by Thomas McQuillan

Figure 24 Dress by Yitzhak Abecassis (2011)/Yitzhak Abecassis

Figure 25 Coat by Simone Austen (2011)/Simone Austen; Pattern by Simone Austen/Simone Austen

Figure 26 Top and skirt by Laura Poole (2010)/Laura Poole; Zero waste t-shirt pattern by Laura Poole (2010)/Laura Poole

Figure 27 Top and skirt by Maja Stabel (2013)/Maja Stabel; Pattern by Maja Stabel (2013)/Maja Stabel

Figure 28 Hierarchy of roles in fashion/Holly McQuillan; Timo Rissanen

Figure 29 Zero Waste organization of roles/Holly McQuillan; Timo Rissanen

Figure 30 Paper figure by Jonathan KYLE Farmer/Jonathan KYLE Farmer

Figure 31A Pyjamas that Timo Rissanen made in 2011 from his grandmother's bedsheets from the 1940s./Timo Rissanen; Photograph by Mariano Garcia

Figure 31B Pattern of pyjamas/Timo Rissanen

Figure 32 Calico toile by Keri Cowdell (left), and Rachel Vickers (right), 2009/Photograph by Kevin Almond

Figure 33A Pattern by Winifred Aldrich/Winifred Aldrich; John Wiley and Sons Limited

Figure 33B Jacket by Winifred Aldrich/Winifred Aldrich; John Wiley and Sons Limited

Figure 34A Pattern by Winifred Aldrich/Winifred Aldrich; John Wiley and Sons Limited

Figure 34B Coat by Winifred Aldrich/Winifred Aldrich; John Wiley and Sons Limited

Figure 35 Dominant approximation of the body for pattern cutting, the tailoring matrix, by Rickard Lindqvist/Rickard Lindqvist

Figure 36 Suggested alternative approximation of the body for pattern cutting, by Rickard Lindqvist/Rickard Lindqvist

Figure 37 Suggested alternative approximation applied on rectangular cut garment, by Rickard Lindqvist/Rickard Lindqvist

Figure 38 Suggested alternative approximation applied on shell jacket pattern, by Rickard Lindqvist/Rickard Lindqvist

Figure 39 Shingo Sato working on a Transformation Reconstruction garment/Shingo Sato

Figure 40 Transformation Reconstruction garment by Shingo Sato/Shingo Sato

Figure 41 Face pattern taped together, by Greg Climer/Greg Climer

Figure 42 Flat pattern for a face by Greg Climer/Greg Climer

Figure 43 (all photos) Pattern cutting process of dress designed through the "Plug" technique by Julian Roberts. A triangle is "plugged" into a shaped hole./Julian Roberts

Figure 44 "Plug" and "Displacement" techniques explained by Roberts during a workshop/Julian Roberts

Figure 45 Julian Roberts' studio, 2014/Julian Roberts

Figure 46A Zero waste, subtraction cut dress by Julian Roberts (2010) can be worn more than seven different ways./Julian Roberts; Photograph by Thomas McQuillan

Figure 46B Julian Roberts (2010) user modifiable zero waste subtraction cut dress, shown in one of its seven iterations/Julian Roberts

Figure 47 Pattern for Roberts' subtraction cut dress for Yield (2010). The arrow shows the direction of the body traveling through the garment./Julian Roberts

Figure 48 Julian Roberts cutting out a Body Ruler, derived from the body of the intended wearer/Julian Roberts; Photograph by Timo Rissanen

Figure 49 Body Ruler used to make sleeve pattern/Julian Roberts

Figure 50 Shirt collaboration by Holly McQuillan and Julian Roberts (2011) using the sleeve pattern cut with the Body Ruler/Pattern and photograph by Holly McQuillan

AQ-18

Learning
Resources
Centre

This book is due for return on or before the last date shown below.

2. May 18

WITHDRAWN